EDGAR WALLACE - THE STANDARD HISTORY OF THE WAR
COMPRISING THE OFFICIAL DESPATCH FROM SIR IAN HAMILTON WITH DESCRIPTIVE MATTER

VOL. IV
THE NAVY AND THE DARDANELLES

Richard Horatio Edgar Wallace was born on the 1st April 1875 in Greenwich, London. Leaving school at 12 because of truancy, by the age of fifteen he had experience; selling newspapers, as a worker in a rubber factory, as a shoe shop assistant, as a milk delivery boy and as a ship's cook.

By 1894 he was engaged but broke it off to join the Infantry being posted to South Africa. He also changed his name to Edgar Wallace which he took from Lew Wallace, the author of *Ben-Hur*.

In Cape Town in 1898 he met Rudyard Kipling and was inspired to begin writing. His first collection of ballads, *The Mission that Failed!* was enough of a success that in 1899 he paid his way out of the armed forces in order to turn to writing full time.

By 1904 he had completed his first thriller, *The Four Just Men*. Since nobody would publish it he resorted to setting up his own publishing company which he called Tallis Press.

In 1911 his Congolese stories were published in a collection called *Sanders of the River*, which became a bestseller. He also started his own racing papers, *Bibury's* and *R. E. Walton's Weekly*, eventually buying his own racehorses and losing thousands gambling. A life of exceptionally high income was also mirrored with exceptionally large spending and debts.

Wallace now began to take his career as a fiction writer more seriously, signing with Hodder and Stoughton in 1921. He was marketed as the 'King of Thrillers' and they gave him the trademark image of a trilby, a cigarette holder and a yellow Rolls Royce. He was truly prolific, capable not only of producing a 70,000 word novel in three days but of doing three novels in a row in such a manner. It was in, estimating that by 1928 one in four books being read was written by Wallace, for alongside his famous thrillers he wrote variously in other genres, including science fiction, non-fiction accounts of WWI which amounted to ten volumes and screen plays. Eventually he would reach the remarkable total of 170 novels, 18 stage plays and 957 short stories.

Wallace became chairman of the Press Club which to this day holds an annual Edgar Wallace Award, rewarding 'excellence in writing'.

Diagnosed with diabetes his health deteriorated and he soon entered a coma and died of his condition and double pneumonia on the 7th of February 1932 in North Maple Drive, Beverly Hills. He was buried near his home in England at Chalklands, Bourne End, in Buckinghamshire.

Index Of Contents

CHAPTER I — THE FIGHT OFF HELIGOLAND

War was declared on August 4 at midnight (German time). At that moment the British fleet, mobilised and ready, was at the stations which had been decided upon in the event of war with Germany. By an act of foresight which cannot be too highly commended the fleet had been mobilised for battle practice a week or so before the actual outbreak of hostilities and at a time when it was not certain whether Great Britain would engage herself in the war. The wisdom of our preparations was seen after war was declared.

From the moment the battle fleet sailed from Spithead and disappeared over the horizon it vanished so far as the average man in the street was concerned, and from that day onward its presence was no more advertised.

The first few days following the outbreak of war we suffered certain losses. On August 6 the Amphion was mined after having destroyed by gun fire the Königin Luise. On September 5 the Pathfinder was torpedoed by a "U" boat, and on September 22 the Aboukir, the Cressy, and the Hogue were destroyed by a German submarine. In the meantime the German had had his trouble. The Magdeburg was shot down by gun fire at the hands of the Russian navy. The Köln, the Ariadne and the Mainz with the German destroyer V187 had been caught in the Bight of Heligoland, and had been sunk.

We had our lessons to learn, and we were prompt to profit by dire experience. The closing of ships to save others had led to the triple disaster of September 22, and save for the vessels we lost in the South Atlantic fight and the two battleships, one of which (Bulwark) was torpedoed and blown up in November, and the other (Formidable) in December, and the blowing up of the Princess Irene in March, we endured no losses in home waters.

In giving a survey of the sea operations one necessarily must deal with those services which are associated with the Navy, and a history of naval matters must necessarily lead to those great operations which developed so sensationally in the Dardanelles and on the Gallipoli Peninsula. It had been hoped that, in the very early stages of the war, the British fleet would be given an opportunity of meeting the German Grand Fleet—a hope foredoomed, since with its marked inferiority it was unlikely that the enemy would try conclusions with his enemy on the sea. Twice did any considerable portion of the enemy fleet venture forth and the thrilling story of the first adventure is told in Vice-Admiral Sir David Beatty's despatch and in the supplementary despatches. The British moved into the Bight of Heligoland on Thursday, August 27, the First Battle Cruiser Squadron and the First Light Cruiser Squadron.

"At 4 a.m., August 28, the movements of the flotillas commenced as previously arranged," wrote Admiral Beatty, "the Battle Cruiser Squadron and Light Cruiser Squadron supporting. The Rear-Admiral, Invincible, with New Zealand and four destroyers having joined my flag, the squadron passed through the pre-arranged rendezvous.

"At 8.10 a.m. I received a signal from the Commodore (1),* informing me that the flotilla was in action with the enemy. This was presumably in the vicinity of their pre-arranged rendezvous. From this time until 11 a.m. I remained about the vicinity ready to support as necessary, intercepting various signals, which contained no information on which I could act."

* Torpedo Boat Destroyer Flotilla.

"At ii a.m. the squadron was attacked by three submarines. The attack was frustrated by rapid manoeuvring, and the four destroyers were ordered to attack them. Shortly after 11 a.m. various signals having been received indicating that the Commodore (1) and Commodore (2)* were both in need of assistance, I ordered the Light Cruiser squadron to support the torpedo flotillas."

* Submarines

"Later I received a signal from the Commodore (I) stating that he was being attacked by a light cruiser, and a further signal informing me that he was being hard pressed and asking for assistance. The Captain (3), First Flotilla, also signalled that he was in need of help.

"From the foregoing the situation appeared to me critical. The flotillas had advanced only ten miles since 8 a.m., and were only about twenty-five miles from two enemy bases on their flank and rear respectively. Commodore Goodenough had detached two of his light cruisers to assist some destroyers earlier in the day, and these had not yet rejoined. (They rejoined at 2.30 p.m.) As the reports indicated the presence of many enemy ships, one a large cruiser, I considered that his force might not be strong enough to deal with the situation sufficiently rapidly, so at 11.30 a.m. the battle cruisers turned to E.S.E., and worked up to full speed. It was evident that to be of any value the support must be overwhelming and carried out at the highest speed possible.

"I had not lost sight of the risk of submarines, and possible sortie in force from the enemy's base, especially in view of the mist to the southeast.

"Our high speed, however, made submarine attack difficult, and the smoothness of the sea made their detection comparatively easy. I considered that we were powerful enough to deal with any sortie except by a battle squadron, which was unlikely to come out in time, provided our stroke was sufficiently rapid.

"At 12.15 p.m. Fearless and First Flotilla were sighted retiring west. At the same time the Light Cruiser Squadron was observed to be engaging an enemy ship ahead. They appeared to have her beat.

"I then steered N.E. to sounds of firing ahead, and at 12.30 p.m. sighted Arethusa and Third Flotilla retiring to the westward engaging a cruiser of the Kolberg class on our port bow. I steered to cut her off from Heligoland, and at 12.37 p.m. opened fire. At 12.42 the enemy turned to N.E., and we chased at 27 knots.

"At 12.56 p.m. sighted and engaged a two-funnelled cruiser ahead. Lion fired two salvoes at her, which took effect, and she disappeared into the mist, burning furiously and in a sinking condition. In view of the mist and that she was steering at high speed at right angles to Lion, who was herself steaming at twenty-eight knots, the Lions firing was very creditable.

"Our destroyers had reported the presence of floating mines to the eastward and I considered it inadvisable to pursue her. It was also essential that the squadron should remain concentrated, and I accordingly ordered a withdrawal. The battle cruisers turned north and circled to port to complete the destruction of the vessel first engaged. She was sighted again at 1.25 p.m. steaming S.E. with colours still flying. Lion opened fire with two turrets, and at 1.35 p.m., after receiving two salvoes, she sank.

"The four attached destroyers were sent to pick up survivors, but I deeply regret that they subsequently reported that they searched the area but found none.

"At 1.40 p.m. the battle cruisers turned to the northward, and Queen Mary was again attacked by a submarine. The attack was avoided by the use of the helm. Lowestoft was also unsuccessfully attacked. The battle cruisers covered the retirement until nightfall. By 6 p.m. the retirement having been well executed and all destroyers accounted for, I altered course, spread the light cruisers, and swept northwards in accordance with the Commander-in-Chiefs orders. At 7.45 p.m. I detached Liverpool to Rosyth with German prisoners, seven officers and seventy-nine men, survivors from Mainz. No further incident occurred."

Of Commodore Tyrwhitt, the Commander of the Destroyer Flotilla, both Rear- Admiral Beatty and Rear-Admiral Christian (commanding the Light Cruiser and Torpedo Boat Destroyer Flotilla), spoke in the most unstinted terms of praise.

"His attack was delivered with great skill and gallantry," says the latter officer.

Admiral Christian also mentioned Commodore Roger T. B. Keyes in Lurcher.

"On the morning of August 28, in company with the Firedrake, he searched the area to the southward of the battle cruisers for the enemy's submarines, and subsequently having been detached, was present at the sinking of the German cruiser Mainz, when he gallantly proceeded alongside her and rescued 220 of her crew, many of whom were wounded. Subsequently he escorted Laurel and Liberty out of action, and kept them company till Rear-Admiral Campbell's cruisers were sighted."

As regards the submarine officers the Admiral specially mentions the names of:—

"Lieutenant-Commander Ernest W. Leir. His coolness and resource in rescuing the crews of the Goshawk's and Defender's boats at a critical time of the action were admirable, and Lieutenant-Commander Cecil P. Talbot. "In my opinion, the bravery and resource of the officers in command of submarines since the war commenced are worthy of the highest commendation."

Commodore Tyrwhitt's story takes us up into the thick of the fight.

"On Thursday, August 27, in accordance with orders received from their lordships, I sailed in Arethusa, in company with the First and Third Flotillas, except Hornet, Tigress, Hydra, and Loyal, to carry out the pre-arranged operations. H.M.S. Fearless joined the flotillas at sea that afternoon.

"At 6.53 a.m. on Friday, August 28, an enemy's destroyer was sighted, and was chased by the fourth division of the Third Flotilla.

"From 7.20 to 7.57 a.m. Arethusa and the Third Flotilla were engaged with numerous destroyers and torpedo boats which were making for Heligoland; course was altered to port to cut them off.

"Two cruisers, with four and two funnels respectively, were sighted on the port bow at 7.57 a.m., the nearest of which was engaged. Arethusareceived a heavy fire from both cruisers and several destroyers until 8.15 a.m., when the four-funnelled cruiser transferred her fire to Fearless.

"Close action was continued with the two-funnelled cruiser on converging courses until 8.25 a.m., when a 6-inch projectile from Arethusa wrecked the forebridge of the enemy, who at once turned away in the direction of Heligoland, which was sighted slightly on the starboard bow at about the same time.

"All ships were at once ordered to turn to the westward, and shortly afterwards speed was reduced to 20 knots.

"During this action Arethusa had been hit many times, and was considerably damaged; only one 6-inch gun remained in action, all other guns and torpedo tubes having been temporarily disabled.

"Lieutenant Eric W. P. Westmacott (Signal Officer) was killed at my side during this action. I cannot refrain from adding that he carried out his duties calmly and collectedly, and was of the greatest assistance to me.

"A fire occurred opposite No. 2 gun port side caused by a shell exploding some ammunition, resulting in a terrific blaze for a short period and leaving the deck burning. This was very promptly dealt with and extinguished by Chief Petty Officer Frederick W. Wrench, O.N. 158,630.

"The flotillas were re-formed in divisions and proceeded at 20 knots. It was now noticed that Arethusa's speed had been reduced.

"Fearless reported that the third and fifth divisions of the First Flotilla had sunk the German Commodore's destroyer and that two boats' crews belonging to Defender had been left behind, as our destroyers had been fired upon by a German cruiser during their act of mercy in saving the survivors of the German destroyer.

"At 10 a.m., hearing that Commodore (S) in Lurcher and Firedrake were being chased by light cruisers, I proceeded to his assistance with Fearless and the First Flotilla until 10.37 a.m., when, having received no news and being in the vicinity of Heligoland, I ordered the ships in company to turn to the westward.

"All guns except two 4-inch were again in working order, and the upper deck supply of ammunition was replenished.

"At 10.55 a.m. a four-funnelled German cruiser was sighted, and opened a very heavy fire about 11 o'clock.

"Our position being somewhat critical, I ordered Fearless to attack, and the First Flotilla to attack with torpedoes, which they proceeded to do with great spirit. The cruiser at once turned away, disappeared in the haze and evaded the attack.

"About ten minutes later the same cruiser appeared on our starboard quarter. Opened fire on her with both 6-inch guns; Fearless also engaged her, and one division of destroyers attacked her with torpedoes without success.

"The state of affairs and our position was then reported to the Admiral commanding Battle Cruiser Squadron.

"We received a very severe and almost accurate fire from this cruiser; salvo after salvo was falling between 10 and 30 yards short, but not a single shell struck; two torpedoes were also fired at us, being well directed, but short.

"The cruiser was badly damaged by Arethusa's 6-inch guns and a splendidly directed fire from Fearless, and she shortly afterwards turned away in the direction of Heligoland.

"Proceeded, and four minutes later sighted the three-funnelled cruiser Mainz. She endured a heavy fire from Arethusa and Fearless and many destroyers. After an action of approximately twenty-five minutes she was seen to be sinking by the head, her engines stopped, besides being on fire.

"At this moment the Light Cruiser Squadron appeared, and they very speedily reduced the Mainz to a condition which must have been indescribable.

"I then recalled Fearless and the destroyers, and ordered cease fire.

"We then exchanged broadsides with a large four-funnelled cruiser on the starboard quarter at long range, without visible effect.

"The Battle Cruiser Squadron now arrived, and I pointed out this cruiser to the Admiral Commanding, and was shortly afterwards informed by him that the cruiser in question had been sunk and another set on fire.

"The weather during the day was fine, sea calm, but visibility poor, not more than three miles at any time when the various actions were taking place, and was such that ranging and spotting were rendered difficult.

"I then proceeded with fourteen destroyers of the Third Flotilla and nine of the First Flotilla. "Arethusa's speed was about six knots until 7 p.m., when it was impossible to proceed any further, and fires were drawn in all boilers except two, and assistance called for.

"At 9.30 p.m. Captain Wilmot S. Nicholson, of the Hogue,* took my ship in tow in a most seamanlike manner, and, observing that the night was pitch dark and the only lights showing were two small hand lanterns, I consider his action was one which deserves special notice from their Lordships.

The Hogue was afterwards destroyed by submarine.

"I would also specially recommend Lieutenant-Commander Arthur P. N. Thorowgood, of Arethusa, for the able manner he prepared the ship for being towed in the dark.

"H.M. ship under my command was then towed to the Nore, arriving at 5 p.m. on August 29. Steam was then available for slow speed, and the ship was able to proceed to Chatham under her own steam.

"I beg again to call attention to the services rendered by Captain W. F. Blunt, of H.M.S. Fearless and the Commanding Officers of the destroyers of the First and Third Flotillas, whose gallant attacks on the German cruisers at critical moments undoubtedly saved Arethusa from more severe punishment and possible capture.

"I cannot adequately express my satisfaction and pride at the spirit and ardour of my officers and ship's company, who carried out their orders with the greatest alacrity under the most trying conditions, especially in view of the fact that the ship, newly built, had not been forty-eight hours out of the Dockyard before she was in action.

"It is difficult to specially pick out individuals, but the following came under my special observation:

H.M.S. Arethusa.
"Lieutenant-Commander Arthur P. N. Thorowgood, First Lieutenant, and in charge of the After Control.
"Lieutenant-Commander Ernest K. Arbuthnot (G), in charge of the Fore Control.
"Sub-Lieutenant Clive A. Robinson, who worked the range-finder throughout the entire action with extraordinary coolness.
"Assistant Paymaster Kenneth E. Badcock, my Secretary, who attended me on the bridge throughout the entire action.
"Mr. James D. Godfrey, Gunner (T), who was in charge of the torpedo tubes.
"The following men were specially noted:
"Armourer Arthur F. Hayes, O.N. 342026 (Ch.).
"Second Sick Berth Steward George Trolley, O.N. M.296 (Ch.).
"Chief Yeoman of Signals Albert Fox, O.N. 194656 (Po.), on fore bridge during entire action.
"Chief Petty Officer Frederick W. Wrench O.N. 158630 (Ch.) (for ready resource in extinguishing fire caused by explosion of cordite).
"Private Thomas Millington, R.M.L.I., No. Ch. 17417.
"Private William J. Beime, R.M.L.I., No. Ch. 13540-
"First Writer Albert W. Stone, O.N. 346080 (Po.).
"I also beg to record the services rendered by the following officers and men of H.M. ships under my orders:

H.M.S. Fearless.
"Mr. Robert M. Taylor, Gunner, for coolness in action under heavy fire.
"The following officers also displayed great resource and energy in effecting repairs to Fearless after her return to harbour, and they were ably seconded by the whole of their staffs:
"Engineer Lieutenant-Commander Charles de F. Messervy.
"Mr. William Morrissey, Carpenter.

H.M.S. Goshawk.
"Commander the Hon. Herbert Meade, who took his division into action with great coolness and nerve, and was instrumental in sinking the German destroyer V187, and, with the boats of his division, saved the survivors in a most chivalrous manner.

H.M.S. Ferret.
"Commander Geoffrey Mackworth, who, with his division, most gallantly seconded Commander Meade, of Goshawk.

H.M.S. Laertes.
"Lieutenant-Commander Malcolm L. Goldsmith, whose ship was seriously damaged, taken in tow, and towed out of action by Fearless.
"Engineer Lieutenant-Commander Alexander Hill, for repairing steering gear and engines under fire.
"Sub-Lieutenant George H. Faulkner, who continued to fight his gun after being wounded.
"Mr. Charles Powell, Acting Boatswain, O.N. 209388, who was gunlayer of the centre gun, which made many hits. He behaved very coolly and set a good example when getting in tow and clearing away the wreckage after the action.

"Edward Naylor, Petty Officer, Torpedo Gunner's Mate, O.N. 189136, who fired a torpedo which the commanding officer of the Laertes reports undoubtedly hit the Mainz, and so helped materially to put her out of action.

"Stephen Pritchard, Stoker Petty Officer, O.N. 285152, who very gallantly dived into the cabin flat immediately after a shell had exploded there, and worked a fire hose.

"Frederick Pierce, Stoker Petty Officer, O.N. 307943, who was on watch in the engine room and behaved with conspicuous coolness and resource when a shell exploded in No. 2 boiler.

H.M.S. Laurel.

"Commander Frank F. Rose, who most ably commanded his vessel throughout the early part of the action, and after having been wounded in both legs, remained on the bridge until 6 p.m., displaying great devotion to duty.

"Lieutenant Charles R. Peploe, First Lieutenant, who took command after Commander Rose was wounded, and continued the action till its close, bringing his destroyer out in an able and gallant manner under most trying conditions.

"Engineer Lieutenant-Commander Edward H. T. Meeson, who behaved with great coolness during the action, and steamed the ship out of action, although she had been very severely damaged by explosion of her own lyddite, by which the after funnel was nearly demolished. He subsequently assisted to carry out repairs to the vessel.

"Sam Palmer, Leading Seaman (G.L. 2) O.N. 179529, who continued to fight his gun until the end of the action, although severely wounded in the leg.

"Albert Edmund Sellens, Able Seaman (L.T.O.), O.N. 217245, who was stationed at the fore torpedo tubes; he remained at his post throughout the entire action, although wounded in the arm, and then rendered first aid in a very able manner before being attended to himself.

"George H. Sturdy, Chief Stoker, O.N. 285547 and

"Alfred Britton, Stoker Petty Officer, O.N. 289893, who both showed great coolness in putting out a fire near the centre gun after an explosion had occurred there; several lyddite shells were lying in the immediate vicinity.

"William R. Boiston, Engine Room Artificer, 3rd class, O.N. M.1369, who showed great ability and coolness in taking charge of the after boiler room during the action, when an explosion blew in the after funnel and a shell carried away pipes and seriously damaged the main steam pipe.

"William H. Gorst, Stoker Petty Officer, O.N. 305616.

"Edward Crane, Stoker Petty Officer, O.N. 307275.

"Harry Wilfred Hawkes, Stoker 1st class, O.N. K.12086.

"John W. Bateman, Stoker 1st class, O.N. K.12100.

"These men were stationed in the after boiler room and conducted themselves with great coolness during the action, when an explosion blew in the after funnel, and shell carried away pipes and seriously damaged the main steam pipe.

H.M.S. Liberty.

"The late Lieutenant-Commander Nigel K. W. Barttelot commanded the Liberty with great skill and gallantry throughout the action. He was a most promising and able officer, and I consider his death is a great loss to the Navy.

"Engineer Lieutenant-Commander Frank A. Butler, who showed much resource in effecting repairs during the action.

"Lieutenant Henry E. Horan, First Lieutenant, who took command after the death of Lieutenant-Commander Barttelot, and brought his ship, out of action in an extremely able and gallant manner under most trying conditions.

"Mr. Harry Morgan, Gunner (T), who carried out his duties with exceptional coolness under fire.

"Chief Petty Officer James Samuel Beadle, O.N. 171735, who remained at his post at the wheel for over an hour after being wounded in the kidneys.

"John Galvin, Stoker Petty Officer, O.N. 279946, who took entire charge, under the Engineer Officer, of the party who stopped leaks, and accomplished his task although working up to his chest in water.

H.M.S. Laforey.
"Mr. Ernest Roper, Chief Gunner, who carried out his duties with exceptional coolness under fire."
The remarkable character of this, the first and certainly the most comprehensive of naval despatches, is that it gives the crew and all branches of the naval service engaged. Battleship cruiser, light cruiser and torpedo boat destroyer alike gave their version and to these may be added the report of Commodore Keyes, who flying his broad pennant on Maidstone, commanded the submarines.

"Three hours after the outbreak of war Submarines E6 (Lieutenant-Commander Cecil P. Talbot) and E8 (Lieutenant-Commander Francis H. H. Goodhart) proceeded unaccompanied to carry out a reconnaissance in the Heligoland Bight. These two vessels returned with useful information, and had the privilege of being the pioneers on a service which is attended by some risk.

"During the transportation of the Expeditionary Force the Lurcher and Firedrake and all the Submarines of the Eighth Submarine Flotilla occupied positions from which they could have attacked the High Sea Fleet had it emerged to dispute the passage of our transports. This patrol was maintained day and night without relief until the personnel of our Army had been transported and all chance of effective interference had disappeared.

"These submarines have since been incessantly employed on the enemy's coast in the Heligoland Bight and elsewhere, and have obtained much valuable information regarding the composition and movement of his patrols. They have occupied his waters and reconnoitred his anchorages, and, while so engaged, have been subjected to skilful and well executed anti-submarine tactics; hunted for hours at a time by torpedo craft and attacked by gunfire and torpedoes.

"At midnight on August 26, I embarked in the Lurcher, and in company with Firedrake and Submarines D2, D8, E4, E5, E6, E7, E8, and E9, of the Eighth Submarine Flotilla, proceeded to take part in the operations in the Heligoland Bight arranged for August 28. The destroyers scouted for the submarines until nightfall on the 27th, when the latter proceeded independently to take up various positions from which they could co-operate with the destroyer flotillas on the following morning.
"At daylight on August 28 the Lurcher and Firedrake searched the area, through which the battle cruisers were to advance, for hostile submarines, and then proceeded towards Heligoland in the wake of Submarines E6, E7, and E8, which were exposing themselves with the object of inducing the enemy to chase them to the westward.*

* It was this daring manoeuvre which induced the German cruisers to move into the open sea.

"On approaching Heligoland, the visibility which had been very good to seaward, reduced to 5,000 to 6,000 yards, and this added considerably to the anxieties and responsibilities of the commanding officers of submarines, who handled their vessels with coolness and judgment in an area which was necessarily occupied by friends as well as foes.

"Low visibility and calm sea are the most unfavourable conditions under which submarines can operate, and no opportunity occurred of closing with the enemy's cruisers to within torpedo range.

"Lieutenant-Commander Ernest W. Leir, commanding Submarine E4, witnessed the sinking of the German Torpedo Boat Destroyer V187 through his periscope, and, observing a cruiser of the Stettin class close, and open fire on the British destroyers which had lowered their boats to pick up the survivors, he proceeded to attack the cruiser, but she altered course before he could get within range. After covering the retirement of our destroyers, which had had to abandon their boats, he returned to the latter, and embarked a lieutenant and nine men of Defender, who had been left behind. The boats also contained two officers and eight men of V187, who were unwounded, and eighteen men who were badly wounded.

"As he could not embark the latter, Lieutenant-Commander Leir left one of the officers and six unwounded men to navigate the British boats to Heligoland. Before leaving he saw that they were provided with water, biscuit, and a compass. One German officer and two men were made prisoners of war.

"Lieutenant-Commander Leir's action in remaining on the surface in the vicinity of the enemy and in a visibility which would have placed his vessel within easy gun range of an enemy appearing out of the mist, was altogether admirable.

"This enterprising and gallant officer took part in the reconnaissance which supplied the information on which these operations were based, and I beg to submit his name and that of Lieutenant-Commander Talbot, the Commanding Officer of E6, who exercised patience, judgment, and skill in a dangerous position, for the favourable consideration of their Lordships.

"On the 13th September E9 (Lieutenant-Commander Max K. Horton) torpedoed and sank the German light cruiser Hela six miles south of Heligoland.*

*Lieut. Max Horton was later to distinguish himself further, for he subsequently torpedoed a big German cruiser in the Baltic "A number of destroyers were evidently called to the scene after E9 had delivered her attack, and these hunted her for several hours.

"On the 14th September, in accordance with his orders, Lieutenant-Commander Horton examined the outer anchorage of Heligoland, a service attended by considerable risk.

"On the 25th September Submarine E6 (Lieutenant-Commander C. P. Talbot), while diving, fouled the moorings of a mine laid by the enemy. On rising to the surface she weighed the mine and sinker; the former was securely fixed between the hydroplane and its guard; fortunately, however, the horns of the mine were pointed outboard. The weight of the sinker made it a difficult and dangerous matter to lift the mine clear without exploding it. After half an hour's patient work this was effected by Lieutenant Frederick A. P. Williams-Freeman and Able Seaman Ernest Randall Cremer, official number 214235, and the released mine descended to its original depth.

"On the 6th October E9 (Lieutenant-Commander Max K. Horton), when patrolling off the Ems, torpedoed and sank the enemy's destroyer Si 26.

"The enemy's torpedo craft pursue tactics which, in connection with their shallow draught, make them exceedingly difficult to attack with torpedo, and Lieutenant-Commander Horton's success was the result of much patient and skilful zeal. He is a most enterprising submarine officer, and I beg to submit his name for favourable consideration.

"Lieutenant Charles M. S. Chapman, the second in command of E9, is also deserving of credit.

"Against an enemy whose capital vessels have never, and light cruisers have seldom, emerged from their fortified harbours, opportunities of delivering submarine attacks have necessarily been few, and on one occasion only, prior to the 13th September, has one of our submarines been within torpedo range of a cruiser during daylight hours.

"During the exceptionally heavy westerly gales which prevailed between the 14th and 21st September the position of the submarines on a lee shore, within a few miles of the enemy's coast, was an unpleasant one.

"The short, steep seas, which accompany westerly gales in the Heligoland Bight, made it difficult to keep the conning tower hatches open. There was no rest to be obtained and even when cruising at a depth of sixty feet the submarines were rolling considerably, and pumping, i.e., vertically moving about twenty feet.

"I submit that it was creditable to the commanding officers that they should have maintained their stations under such conditions.

"Service in the Heligoland Bight is keenly sought after by the commanding officers of the eighth submarine flotilla, and they have all shown daring and enterprise in the execution of their duties. These officers have unanimously expressed to me their admiration of the cool and gallant behaviour of the officers and men under their command. They are, however, of the opinion that it is impossible to single out individuals when all have performed their duties so admirably, and in this I concur."

CHAPTER II — THE OUTER FLEETS

There are things that must always be remembered, in estimating the work of the Navy. There are the peculiar nature of the task allotted to the Navy, the part it was expected to play in bringing about the end of the enemy's resistance, the difficulties and the enormous dangers it was called upon to share. These things considered, when we ask ourselves if the British Navy had carried out its part of the contract in the great war, there can be no other answer than an emphatic affirmative. We were not fighting the German Navy, we were fighting the German nation.- Sheltered behind the men doing their splendid work up and down the seas were millions of people who looked to them for assistance in carrying out their daily avocations. They looked to the sea to bring them the means of livelihood, the raw materials to fashion into finished products, the coal, the iron ores, the fabrics, or the raw material of fabrics, and, vitally necessary, food to sustain life within the Empire.

Countries cannot live on themselves under modern economic conditions. They must have customers and clients to whom they must have access. When neither raw material is coming in nor completed manufacture going out, factories close down, many people are thrown out of employment, and labourers who were till then not only self-sustaining but were helping in the larger business of upholding the State, become a burden upon the nation.

So that, since Germany depended very largely upon seaborne trade, and since all her land borders save one were in the hands of the enemy, it is not difficult to understand the first duty of the Navy and the paramount importance of the task which was set for Admiral Jellicoe. It was a task which meant a constant hazardous patrolling and a continuous search of ships, neutral as well as enemy, since it has been found, and has been proved during the present war, that the German secured most of his advantages under a flag which was not his.

All this and more the Navy did, in its unwinking watch over the seas. Daily, hourly, our Navy spelt out the far-reaching significance of sea-power. In addition to its ceaseless patrolling, its tireless searching, which means the strangle-hold upon the trading of our enemy, it convoyed the great transports, with their war-material of men and guns, from the far places of the Empire.

It was not to be expected that its work could be carried on without mishap. Mine and raiding submarine were constantly at work against our ships. The nature of the work the Navy had to do made it, as it were, an enormous target for the enemy. Our own submarines had little chance of retaliating in like manner, for the German Navy lay behind the bolted doors of its secure harbours. Later in the book is given a comparative list of disasters on the British and the German sides, up to the end of the first year of war. It will help the reader to understand the character of the naval war. It was of a character inevitable so far as our Navy was concerned.

The D5 was sunk as the aftermath of a visit of four German cruisers to our shores. A coastguard gunboat, the Halcyon, was engaged in patrolling early one misty morning, off Lowestoft, when the enemy's cruisers appeared. They fired several shots, damaging the Halcyon's wireless, and then made a prompt retreat at full speed. Although shadowed by some of our light cruisers, they could not be brought to action before dusk, and our pursuit was abandoned. One of these fleeing cruisers threw out a number of mines, and submarine D5 was sunk by exploding one of these.

It was afterwards learnt that the Yorck, a German cruiser which was presumably one of the squadron that had taken part in this spectacular but ineffective raid, had sunk owing to collision with one of the mines guarding Wilhelmshaven.

Of all the German ships the Emden gained the greatest notoriety, and it is a commentary upon the character of the British race that, in spite of the enormous amount of damage which the Emden did to British shipping, she paralysed the East Indian trade for over a month, the British people heartily admired the skill and courage of her Commander and crew, and paid willing tribute to the courtesy which Captain von Muller invariably showed to those who unfortunately came across the Emden's path.

When war broke out the Emden, a light armoured cruiser, was stationed at Kiao-chau, and possibly the inevitability of Japan joining in caused the German Admiralty to detach this light, fast cruiser to her work of destruction. Attended by colliers, she disappeared from the China seas, and reappeared in the Indian Ocean on September 10th.

The greater portion of the British fleet was at that time engaged in convoying the Indian contingent to Europe, so that the Captain of the Emden knew that he might with impunity come prowling through the Indian seas on the off-chance of picking up a few stray merchantmen. In this surmise he was justified, for in four days he had captured and sunk six merchant ships, removing their crews before sending the vessels to the bottom. On the 22nd the Emden suddenly appeared before Madras, and with an audacity worthy of the best traditions of the British Navy— upon which the German Navy was modelled—she bombarded this important Indian town, doing no more damage, however, than setting fire to a number of oil tanks. The time was night, and the bombardment only lasted for a quarter of an hour. Again she vanished, and news came of her in the Indian Ocean, where she went to work capturing and sinking the British merchantmen that came her way. An instance of Captain von Muller's humanity is cited in the case of the Kabinga. Yon Muller had intended sinking this vessel, when he found that the captain's wife was on board. He personally interviewed the lady.
"
I cannot send you adrift in an open boat," he said with a twinkle in his eye, "so you must go back to England and tell the owners of the Kabinga that she is to be regarded as having been captured and sunk. . I present the ship to you."

And thus with a laugh he spared the boat.

In the middle of October H.M.S. Yarmouth, which had been ceaselessly searching for this pest of the ocean, came upon the Hamburg-Amerika liner Marcomania, and a Greek steamer which had been accompanying theEmden and carrying coal and ammunition for the vessel.

These two ships were promptly sunk by the British Commander, who could not afford at the moment to put a prize crew on board and send them into port. Undoubtedly this was a very great blow to the Emden; but between that period and October 22 she had sunk five more ships in the south-west.

The Admiralty recognised the feeling of unrest and insecurity which the presence of this ship created, and there was a concentration of fast cruisers, including French, Russian, and Japanese working in harmony with His Majesty's Australian ships Melbourne and Sydney, to search out and sink this danger to British commerce. Before she was captured, however, the Emden was to embark upon her last and most daring exploit.

Rigging an extra funnel to disguise herself, she steamed boldly into the roadstead at Penang, where there lay at anchor a Russian cruiser and a French destroyer. The new vessel's arrival was sighted by the officer of the watch on the Russian cruiser, and an interrogatory signal was flown to which the Emden replied "Yarmouth coming to an anchor." She came at full speed into the roadstead, and before anybody could realise what was happening she had slipped two torpedoes at the Russian, and then, as the French destroyer moved up to attack, she opened fire with both broadsides upon her two unprepared enemies, and sunk them at their moorings.

Nemesis was on her track, however. She went into Keeling Cocos Island with the object of destroying the wireless apparatus in that isolated spot, and the telegraph operator, recognising her, flashed out a warning signal which was picked up by the Minotaur and transmitted to H.M.S. Sydney.

The Emden landed a party which destroyed the instruments; but in the midst of their work of destruction the Emden's siren called them back. Before the landing party could reach the boat she was under way, for on the horizon loomed the grey hull of the Sydney, and her guns were already getting the range. The Emden's two funnels were shot away and she ran ashore, burning fiercely aft. Her losses were very heavy. The superior range of the Sydney's guns enabled the Commander of the Australian ship severely to damage his enemy without himself coming into range, except at the beginning of the action, when a well- placed shot by the Emden destroyed the range-finding apparatus and killed three men.

Simultaneously with the publication of this fine exploit came the news, no less encouraging, that another of the German commerce destroyers, the Königsberg, had been located up an East African river, and had been bottled up by the sinking of a collier in the fairway. The Königsberg was the ship which bombarded the Pegasus while it lay at anchor at Zanzibar.

In the Pacific a serious action off the coast of Chili resulted in our losing two cruisers, the Good Hope (the flagship of the Pacific Squadron) and the Monmouth. They tackled a superior concentration of German ships, including the Scharnhorst and the Gneisenau, which were lucky in having far heavier armament than the British ships possessed. The Glasgow survived and reached Valparaiso to tell the story of the unequal combat, Captain John Luce, of the Glasgow, having told the following story, a thrilling record of a gallant losing fight:—

"2 p.m.—Flagship signalled that apparently from wireless calls there was an enemy ship to northward. Orders were given for squadron to spread N.E. by E. in the following order:—Good Hope, Monmouth, Otranto and Glasgow, speed to be worked up to 15 knots.

"4.20 p.m.—Saw smoke; proved to be enemy ships, one small cruiser and two armoured cruisers. Glasgow reported to Admiral, ships in sight were warned and all concentrated on Good Hope.

"5.47 p.m.—Squadron formed in line ahead in following order: Good Hope, Monmouth, Glasgow, Otranto. Enemy, who had turned south, were now in single line ahead, 12 miles off, Scharnhorst and Gneisenau leading.

"6.18 p.m.—Speed ordered to 17 knots, and flagship signalled Canopus: 'I am going to attack enemy now.' Enemy were now 15,000 yards away, and maintained this range, at the same time jambing wireless signals. By this time sun was setting immediately behind us from enemy position . . . and while it remained above horizon we had advantage in light, but range too great.

"6.55 p.m.—Sun set, and visibility conditions altered, our ships being silhouetted against afterglow, and failing light made enemy difficult to see.

"7.3 p.m.—Enemy opened fired 12,000 yards, followed in quick succession by Good Hope, Monmouth, Glasgow. Two squadrons were now converging, and each ship engaged opposite number in the line. Growing darkness and heavy spray of head sea made firing difficult, particularly for main deck guns of Good Hope and Monmouth. Enemy firing salvoes got range quickly, and their third salvo caused fire to break out on fore part of both ships, which were constantly on fire till 7.45 p.m.

"7.50 p.m.—Immense explosion occurred on Good Hope amidships, flames reaching 200 feet high. Total destruction must have followed. It was now quite dark. Both sides continued firing at flashes of opposing guns. Monmouth was badly down by the bow and turned away to get stern to sea, signalling to Glasgow to that effect.

"8.30 p.m.—Glasgow signalled to Monmouth 4 enemy following us,' but received no reply. Under rising moon, enemy's ships were now seen approaching, and as Glasgow could render Monmouth no assistance, she proceeded at full speed to avoid destruction.

"8.50 p.m.—Lost sight of enemy.

"9.20 p.m.—Observed seventy-five flashes of fire, which was no doubt final attack on Monmouth. "Nothing could have been more admirable than the conduct of officers and men throughout. Though it was most trying to receive a great volume of fire without chance of returning it adequately, all kept perfectly cool, there was no wild firing, and discipline was the same as at battle practice.

"When target ceased to be visible gun-layers spontaneously ceased fire.

"The serious reverse sustained has entirely failed to impair the spirit of officers and ships company, and it is our unanimous wish to meet the enemy again as soon as possible."

Admiral Cradock, who commanded the British squadron, had undoubtedly a force wholly inadequate to deal with the German vessels, should they decide upon a combination. The Scharnhorst and Gneisenau were superior to any ship which the British admiral had in his squadron, though the Good Hope could boast of two 9 2 guns, as against the 8-inch batteries of the enemy. But the 9 2, admirable weapon as it was in the days when it was the pet gun of the Navy, is a type of gun which was modern—twenty years ago. If you eliminate the 9'2 guns, then the British ships were at a great disadvantage to their enemy; for between them the German carried sixteen 8 2 guns, and no fewer than seventy-two smaller pieces ranging from 3*4 up to 5*9, as against the two 9'2 and forty-two other guns varying from 4-inch to 6-inch. The Scharnhorst and Gneisenau were two of the newest ships that Germany had launched, whilst on the other hand the Good Hope was a fifteen year old boat, and her main deck guns were so placed that in a heavy sea they were almost awash.

Recognising something of the danger, the Admiralty had detached an old battleship, the Canopus, to act with Admiral Cradock, but she unfortunately was without speed, though she carried 12-inch guns, which would give the British Squadron superiority over the enemy. The Canopus had not arrived, though it was apparently within signalling distance, on November 1st, when the Good Hope, sweeping slowly down the stormy sea off the south-west coast of South America, picked up a suspicious wireless message which suggested that an enemy warship was somewhere in the vicinity. The flagship sent a wireless to the Monmouth, the Otranto (a converted liner) and the Glasgow, to concentrate at a given point; and at half-past four that afternoon the British squadron, labouring through a heavy sea with a northerly gale, increasing every moment until it was almost a hurricane, blowing on their quarter, sighted smoke on the horizon, and presently made out a small cruiser and two armoured cruisers. Admiral Cradock's position was a dangerous one. He could recognise the gun superiority of his enemy. He could not afford to wait for the Canopus, a slow ship, nor could he afford again to lose sight of his elusive enemy. He signalled to form line ahead, and with the flagship leading, followed by the Monmouth, Glasgow, and Otranto, the squadron steamed inward, drawing closer every minute to the enemy. Both fleets were steaming in the same direction, and both altered their course inward to bring them together. It was a wild and impressive scene, that November night; the great, green waves, mountain high, the squadrons wallowing and rolling through the tumbling ocean, their decks awash and green sea sweeping over them. The sun was setting redly in the west, and the afterglow threw the ships of the British squadron into high relief, leaving the enemy veiled in the grey of the coming night. At seven o'clock fire was opened at 12,000 yards by the enemy, and the Good Hope, Monmouth, and Glasgowinstantly came into action, the squadrons converging. The conditions were abnormal. Around the guns the men slipped and staggered as the shuddering vessels sunk and rose in the trough of the sea, and the icy blast of the hurricane shrieked along the unprotected decks and blinded the gunners with spray. Too soon the enemy's salvoes found their mark, and one of the 9*2 guns, which represented the only hope the British squadron had of outmatching the enemy, was put out of action a few minutes after the fight began.

With her smaller guns awash, with her big guns out of action, the Good Hope was a target for the great German cruisers to pound. Neither the Monmouth nor the Good Hope could make effective reply, and after half-an-hour of this unequal fight, both ships burning fore and aft, the Good Hope blew up amidships and went down in the dark. The Glasgow now moved off.

As we have seen by her Captain's despatch, she could render no assistance to the unfortunate Monmouth. This ship, with a bad list and making water rapidly, suddenly turned, signalling to the Glasgow to make for safety. "I am going to try to ram one of them," was her laconic signal, and that, and the stabbing pencils of gun fire in the dark, were all that the Glasgow could see of the doomed ship. Her gallant crew went to their death in a super-heroic attempt to destroy their enemy even in their last throes. Not a soul was saved from either the Monmouth or Good Hope.

In that action the German ships engaged were the Gneisenau and the Scharnhorst, with the smaller Nürnberg. Both from the official account and from that supplied by eye-witnesses of the the fight, it does not seem that any other German vessel took part, and possibly the claim that the Nürnberg was the ship that gave the Monmouth her quietus was justified. Such a reverse, coming on the top of the success we had gained against the Emden, had a dispiriting effect, but the Admiralty acted with commendable promptitude. There was at Whitehall at this time Admiral Sturdee, who was acting as Chief of Staff to Lord Fisher. With no delay whatever he left his office chair, and, after the briefest instructions, journeyed to a certain port where the nucleus of a new fleet was waiting, and hoisting his flag, set his squadron's bows direct for the eastern coast of South America.

We may suppose that the Japanese Fleet, already scouring the Pacific, were moving up in strength to force the enemy to leave the western waters. It is known that the Scharnhorst, Gneisenau, Nürnberg, Dresden and Leipzig rounded the Cape of Good Hope and moved up to that rendezvous where their colliers and their supplies were waiting. But within six weeks of their victory they paid the price.

It was a very strong squadron that Admiral Sturdee commanded, including the big battle cruisers, Invincible and Inflexible. On December 7th the British ships arrived at Port Stanley to coal, leaving the Canopus on guard outside the harbour. A fine intelligence system served Admiral Sturdee well, for on the very next day the German squadron under Admiral von Spee appeared (doubtless with the intention of seizing the islands and provisioning his ships) and, seeing only the Canopus—an easy prey—advanced at once to the attack. Swiftly he discovered the trap laid for him, but not swiftly enough, for it was too late to run when the other British ships appeared and gave battle.

Since his defeat of Sir Christopher Cradock's squadron, von Spee had been harassed by the knowledge that English and Japanese ships were sweeping eastward in pursuit of him. But it is probable that he had been fairly confident that no new danger would threaten him from the Atlantic. Now, to his surprise, he had to face Sturdee's ships, their crews hot to avenge their fallen comrades.

From the beginning there could only be one end to the encounter. But von Spee, heavily over-matched, fought bravely on his flagship, upon which the British vessels at first concentrated their fire. At the end of an hour she began to settle, but she refused to surrender; at last her bow lifted out of the water, there was a great coughing of steam, and she went down with all on board. With the Gneisenau and the Leipzig it was the same.

The battle was not of long duration. The Scharnhorst, Gneisenau and Leipzig were shot down with a loss to the Germans of probably 1,800 men, and the Nürnberg and Dresden utilising their great speed, sought to escape. This the Dresden succeeded in accomplishing, for she was three knots faster than her unfortunate companion. The Nürnberg, chased by fast cruisers, was destroyed by shell fire, and the Dresden slipped her pursuers, only to avert the evil day of her destruction, which from the first was inevitable.

Thus ended the great adventure which had begun with the declaration of war. It had seen the destruction of the Scharnhorst, Gneisenau, Emden, Leipzig, Nürnberg, and the bottling up of the Königsberg. Of the ships which Germany had sent out to harass the commerce of the Allies, only Karlsruhe and Dresden remained. Karlsruhe subsequently blew up whilst Dresden was finally brought to bay off the coast of Chili.

CHAPTER III — NORTH SEA BRUSHES

Throughout the war there was a certain co-ordination between the land and sea forces of the Crown which was apparent even to those unimaginative people who might not see at first glance what association there was between the destruction of von Spee's squadron and the safety of our army in France. Yet that association was very real. Sometimes the events on land had a very real connection with the naval position and in one case, the employment of the Monitors Severn and Mersey to shell the German trenches near Lombartzyde, the cooperation was expressed in a visible shape.

Toward the end of November the enemy was becoming desperate. The exhilaration which had been created in Berlin by the sinking of the Good Hope and the Monmouth off the coast of Chile, and by the victory which Germany had claimed to have inflicted upon the Russians, was replaced by a sense of depression and bitter chagrin when the news came that the fine Southern Pacific Squadron of the German Navy had been wiped out by Admiral Sturdee near the Falkland Islands. Add to this the fact that day after day had passed without any confirmation being received of the success which was supposed to have attended von Hindenburg's efforts against Warsaw, and you may realise something of that wave of impotent rage which swept across Germany, and induced the Great General Staff to find some desperate method of reviving the flagging spirits of the German people. It was no heroic method that was chosen, no exploit undertaken which will live in German history as a deed of incomparable daring. Rather it is one of which the German will, in years to come, be loth to speak. On the night of November 15th five cruisers slipped out of Wilhelmshaven in the dark.

Three of these were battle cruisers and two were light, unarmoured vessels; but all had the advantage of immense speed. A thick mist lay on the water, as with every light extinguished and steaming line ahead, the battle cruisers leading, the German fleet went at full speed westward. The journey was fraught with many dangers. British submarines and torpedo boats were patrolling the outer circle of German waters; cruisers were everywhere on the look-out for stray enemy craft. But the German evidently moved with complete confidence, for he was in possession of all the information he required as to the movements and the exact location of every British vessel. The system of espionage which had been going on in England ever since the war started served him in excellent stead. Not so excellent, however, but that the British Fleet learned at midnight that four or five vessels had succeeded in making their escape through the cordon, and in the early hours of the morning British battleship cruisers moved stealthily out from their bases and began to search the wide space of ocean for their enemy.

Seeking for enemy ships by night is a difficult matter under the most favourable circumstances. Looking for him in the early hours of that morning, when a sea fog covered the face of the water, was well-nigh hopeless.

Scarborough, the queen of British watering places, might well imagine war to be remote and apart from its own quiet, suave existence. People woke between seven and eight to a grey dawn and a thin driving mist, and may have felt some sense of satisfaction and pride when through the sea three great men-of-war came stealing cautiously towards the land. Scarborough itself, or such of Scarborough as was awake at that moment, had no doubt in its mind that these ships were British men-of-war. They had seen them before. The advent of battleships and cruisers was no new experience, and the few idlers on the sea front who were abroad at that hour speculated upon the names of these great grey shapes.

Then without warning the three ships belched fire. A strange new sound came to the peaceful people of the Yorkshire town. The dreadful scream of shell; the crashing of high explosives as the shells reached their objective; the frenzied cries of women struck down by murderous salvoes; the roar and tear of shattered buildings; the crashing of falling masonry; all these things told too plainly the almost unbelievable news that Scarborough, peaceful, unarmed and undefended, was the object of a German attack.

The raid itself, of course, had no military value whatever. So far from shaking the faith of the British, either in the justice of their cause or in the inevitability of their victory, the attack resulted in a great increase of recruits, for it brought home to even the most laggard of our fellow countrymen the realisation of the length to which the German would go to secure his ends. In a letter to the Mayor of Scarborough, Mr. Winston Churchill the First Lord of the Admiralty, designated the German squadron as baby-killers, and as baby-killers they will be remembered to the end of their days. The ignobility of the attack is, as I say, made evident by the complete suppression of the names of the ships which took part in the raid. It was not a matter of which any German sailor can be proud. There was an additional reason for secrecy to be found in the possibility of drastic reprisal if ever the captains of these ships fell into British hands.

CHAPTER IV — DESTRUCTION OF THE BLÜCHER

The Scarborough raid, hailed with joy in Germany as an indication of Britain's inability to keep the seas, was successful only by the greatest of flukes. The British Admiralty had ample warning of the German intention, but their information led them to believe that the objective of the German Fleet was another part of the coast. To meet this raid a considerable force had been got together. When news came that the German had changed his plans and that he was already bombarding Scarborough, the Fleet set off with all haste to intercept the enemy, and would have succeeded in this object but for the fact that utilising a friendly fog bank, the German Fleet disappeared into the mist and made its escape.

The British Admiralty were equally well informed as to the departure of a Fleet which left Cuxhaven after dark on Saturday, January 23rd, and steamed slowly westward. It consisted of Derfflinger, Seydlitz, Moltke, Blücher, a number of small cruisers, including Kolberg, and a fleet of submarines and destroyers. When the news was received that this fleet was on its way, the British Battle Cruiser Squadron, under Admiral Sir David Beatty, consisting of Lion (flagship), Tiger, Princess Royal, New Zealand, and Indomitable, accompanied by a number of small craft, moved out to intercept the marauder, who was setting his course probably for Newcastle.

The composition of the enemy's squadron was interesting. Derfflinger was a brand-new ship, laid down only eighteen months previously and only completed for sea in November, 1914. She was perhaps the most powerful of Germany's battle cruisers. Moltke was a sister ship to Goeben, the Dreadnought cruiser which escaped our Fleet in the Mediterranean and ran for safety to the Dardanelles, afterwards being taken over by the Turk. Seydlitz was a very fast and powerful battle cruiser; Blücher was a ship which was laid down in error, the Germans having received inaccurate information as to our ship-building intentions and having built Blücher with the idea of going one better than a mysterious ship which the British were building in one of the dockyards. That ship, as it happened, was Dreadnought, which, because of its size and its armaments, entirely negatived this effort of the German Admiralty, and established a new model for the world.

On the British side, Lion, a very powerful Dreadnought cruiser, was remarkable for its great speed. Tigerwas not ready for the sea when war broke out, but Princess Royal, New Zealand and Indomitable had all seen much sea service. Of these five Indomitable was the slowest. Cooperating with the battle-cruiser fleet was a destroyer flotilla, under Commodore Tyrwhitt who carried into action Arethusa and Undaunted, two ships which had already made their mark in the naval history of the war.

Unaware of the preparations which were being made to receive him, the German Admiral (probably Admiral Funke) came swiftly through the night, having distributed his instructions to his captains as to their objective. There is not much reason to doubt that that objective was again the undefended coast line.

The Marconi signallers on the German battleships, with their ear-pieces strapped to their heads, listened intently for any errant signal which would betray the presence of British warships. One signal alone came to them—the signal of a patrolling warship which was at that moment communicating with the shore a request concerning the domestic economy of the ship. Such a message was immensely gratifying to the German Admiral, who found in this innocent communication support for his faith in British unpreparedness.

The shock came at a little after seven in the morning, when, on the horizon, his look-out detected five pillars of misty smoke at suspiciously regular intervals. A scrutiny of these satisfied the German Admiral as to their nature. A string of signals fluttered up to his mainmast, and in obedience, this mighty fleet of Germany immediately swung round and headed for home with all speed.

At this time the ships of the British Fleet were not even visible to the naked eye. They were, indeed, no more than a blur of dun-coloured smoke upon the horizon, but the German Admiral, through his telescope, had been able to make out the composition of the force which was opposing him, and he was quite satisfied that discretion should be the better part of his valour.

Then ensued a thrilling flight, demoralising to the pursued, exhilarating to the pursuer, as every hour brought him nearer to his enemy. It was a pursuit carried out at first in silence, unbroken by roar of guns; a pursuit which was written in belching smoke that curled and trailed upon the dark green waters, and in the white fan of the flying warships' wake. Thirty miles had been covered by the racing ships, and the nearest British vessel was all but ten miles away when there came the first low rumbling thunder of the mighty British guns, and the shriek of a great shell. It struck the rearmost vessel, the Blacker, the slowest of the enemy fleet, and sent splinters of red-hot shell flying in all directions. It was followed instantly by another, and yet another; and then, as the British crept up hand over hand, the target was shifted from the rearmost ship, and Lion, leading the battle line, began dropping her shells upon Moltke and Seydlitz.

Moving at tremendous rates so that the two foremost British ships, Lion and Tiger, were well clear of their fellows these two began a continuous fire from their forward batteries, until at last they drew within long range of Derfflinger, and brought the whole of the German battle fleet under fire. And the German clapped on speed in his flight for home and the shelter of his mine field.
Back and forward went the quick exchange, Tiger engaging three ships at once, whilst the other ships of the line, Princess Royal, Indomitable and New Zealand, drew up to Blücher, which was now on fire fore and aft.

On Indomitable, the last of the line, the excitement had been intense. Would the slowest of the battle cruisers get up in time to join the fight? The stokers off duty ("the black squad ") settled that point. They volunteered to go down and assist their brethren in the deeps of the stokehole, that Indomitable might not be last in the hunt.

Stripped to the waist and tingling with joyful excitement they stoked Indomitable to such purpose that she pulled out four knots more than she had achieved upon her trials. And now the reward came. A signal to Indomitable, brief and to the point, "Settle Blücher!" brought this fine ship into action.

Blücher had heeled over and drawn out of the line, her fore turrets swept away, her bridge vanished, her steel tripod masts a mass of wreckage. With funnels battered and hanging limply, scarred and holed above and below water-line, she wallowed in the trough of the sea, still firing her guns desperately. Every British ship that passed her gave her one salvo, for she had been the craft which had begun the bombardment of Scarborough and the British gunners were saying "Remember Scarborough" as they fired. The end came when Tiger and Indomitable addressed themselves to the business of finishing Blücher for good.

Whilst this was going on, the German ships were rapidly approaching the mined sea area which had been prepared for such a contingency, a field lying fifty miles to the west of Heligoland. Here mines were thickly sown, and only ships having a complete knowledge of their position could be safe here. It became evident to Sir David Beatty that he must break off action in a very short time, and he renewed his efforts to cripple the remainder of the German Fleet. Manoeuvring his ships so that he veiled them from the German gunners in the smoke which was pouring from the enemy's funnels, he drew closer, and the forward guns of Lion and Tiger thundered incessantly. The scene upon the battered German warships was indescribable. The shock and crash of exploding shells, which swept huge guns from their mountings as though they were toys, which destroyed men so that nothing was left of them, which made the very steel decks red-hot, drove some men mad.

Derfflinger was on fire forward, and flames were leaping up as high as the mainmast. Men from all the German ships were throwing themselves overboard, trusting to the hope of being rescued rather than to enduring that hell any longer. Moltke and Seydlitz, with fires blazing fore and aft, with the merciless shells dropping left and right, were in deplorable condition.

Then Lion met bad luck. A lucky shot fired by Seydlitz struck one of the feed tanks of the flagship and caused her to reduce speed, and at the same time enemy submarines were sighted to starboard of her. The German ships had reached the outer ring of the mine defences—a defence which they had elongated by the process of dropping overboard a number of mines in their flight. On the edge of the minefield lay the submarines, waiting their chance to defend the battleships; and when Sir David Beatty, realising that he had reached the margin of safety, decided to break off the action, these came out to attack Lion. Steaming with one engine, Lion steered to the north-west, and Admiral Beatty transferred his flag to one of the destroyers, and subsequently to Princess Royal. The starboard engines of Lionnow began to give trouble, and Indomitable took her in tow and brought her safely into port.

Now on the fringe of the minefield, with the advent of the strong submarine flotilla that had come out from Heligoland, the British Fleet was in danger. The long line of British destroyers which had been racing in the wake of the battle cruisers came up, and quickly assumed a formation which put them into a circle, the centre of which was the battle cruisers. Round and round at top speed the destroyers raced, ever widening their circle and ever keeping at a distance the baffled submarines. The great speed of the torpedo boat destroyer as compared with the slow-moving submarine rendered any possibility of attack upon the battle cruisers futile.

Other destroyers, standing by the place where Blücher had sunk, picked up as many of the exhausted men of that ship as they could, despite the operations of a German airship circling overhead, which, all the time, was attempting to drop bombs upon the rescuing destroyers. Many of the men who were saved were in the last stages of exhaustion. Some were suffering from most terrible injuries; others were mad.

The captain of Blacker was taken on board one of the rescuing ships in a state of utter collapse.*

He subsequently died in hospital.

In the morning these great cruisers of ours had trembled to the shock of explosions, and watchful men, in the dark, close confines of steel turrets, had worked their destructive guns. In the afternoon these same British sailors, relentless and remorseless, were searching their kits to provide clothing for the half-drowned, wholly chilled and utterly unnerved members of the enemy crews.

It was learned from the rescued men that the German Navy had sustained another complete loss. The Kolberg, one of the light cruisers, acting on the flank of the bigger ships, had been struck by over-salvoes which had passed their objective—the battle cruisers—and had sunk the smaller vessel. The German prisoners were agreed that she went down—a fact which the German Admiralty eventually denied.

It was a significant circumstance, which has been insufficiently commented upon, that the prisoners taken from the water consisted of representatives from all the ships of the flying German Fleet. In other words, the conditions had been so terrible upon the German warships which had escaped sinking, that men preferred death under the open sky and in the sea of icy water to a chance of life on these stricken ships.

Thus ended the second attempt of the German to reach the British coast, an attempt as ignoble in conception as it was disastrous in result. Our losses were: Lion, 17 wounded; Tiger, one officer and nine men killed, three officers and eight men wounded; Meteor, four men killed and one man wounded. The enemy losses were two ships and about 800 men. It was necessary to tow Lion and Meteor out of the area, but nearer to port Lion had sufficiently recovered to be able to come into harbour under her own steam. The injuries to the ships themselves were unimportant.

The battle was fought on Sunday, January 24, between the hours of 7.30 and 3 o'clock.

CHAPTER V — THE NAVAL AIRMEN

The work of the British airmen, both naval and army branches, was consistently excellent throughout, and as time went on, the British flying man, capable, resourceful, and daring, acquired ascendancy over his German rival. It is more convenient to deal first with the exploits of the naval branch of our air service.

Royal Naval airmen had accomplished a daring flight to Düsseldorf, destroying the Zeppelin shed there and with it one of the newest Zeppelins; and the success of that raid struck something like dismay into German hearts. The temper of the German people, which is represented in all the official accounts as steady and calm and most admirably confident, may best be gauged from the fact that it was necessary for the Military Commander at Cologne to issue special orders and injunctions to soothe the panic-stricken population, which for twenty years or more has been persistently told that, whatever might be the result of a war in which Germany was engaged, it was certain that the people of the interior towns would never hear the sound of a shot fired by an enemy.

The Zeppelin threat was one which had been held over Great Britain, not so much, one imagines, to terrorise our people as to keep the German folk in good heart.

The headquarters of the Zeppelin industry were at Friedrichshafen, on Lake Constance and it was known in the early days of November that two or three new Zeppelins were in course of manufacture at this place. Three British airmen decided upon the most daring raid that the war so far had produced. This was none other than an attempt to reach Friedrichsfaven from the French frontier and to destroy the Zeppelins in course of construction.

Three well-known men in the Naval Air Service were chosen for the work— Squadron Commander Briggs, Flight-Commander Babington and Flight-Lieutenant Sippe. Squadron Commander Briggs was one of the best air pilots we have had, a man who had put up the British altitude record to 15,000 feet.

The attempt involved a considerable amount of preparation, a very careful study of maps, and a reconnaissance, as far as it was possible to make one, for the first hundred miles of the flight. The statement made by Germany that our airmen were aided by information improperly conveyed by our diplomatic representatives in Switzerland needs no confutation. We had fought always with clean hands, and we had never yet utilised the territory or the sympathy of neutrals in order to secure our ends. This is not a claim which can be repeated with any truth by our enemy.

The attempt was made from Belfort, and early one grey morning, in the presence of the superior officers of the French garrison, who were the only people in the secret, the three gallant Britons began their flight. It was a flight without parallel in the history of this war, which has produced so many precedents. It carried the aviators over wild country, across high mountains, where every care had to be taken that the neutrality of Switzerland was not violated. For in these days nations claim the air as their territory just as assuredly as they claim the land below. The weather was intensely cold, and the gallant British airmen encountered, in one period of their flight, a very strong wind which caused them no little anxiety, threatening as it did the untimely termination of this adventure.

One of the aviators lost his way in a bank of cloud just before the objective was reached, and emerged to see Commander Briggs, shot at by anti-aircraft guns and shelled in all directions, making a steep dive down to the air shed where the new Zeppelin was building. Then, and only then, when he was sure of his ground, did Commander Briggs drop his terrible bombs. There was a burst of flame and smoke, but, undeterred, the second airman came swooping down in that inferno and dropped other bombs to complete the attack. In wide circles the aviators came back to their elevation, the wings of their machines riddled by rifle and shrapnel shot. Briggs alone fell, but steadied his flight and landed with little or no injury. For a few moments he was surrounded by an angry crowd, but a pointed revolver kept them at a respectful distance, until, on the arrival of an officer with some soldiers, the gallant Commander surrendered. It is reported, and we can only hope that the story is unfounded, that when the German officer discovered that the revolver with which the airman had been threatening his men was unloaded, he lashed his prisoner across the face with a riding whip.

The perils of his two companions were not at an end. If they had come unperceived, they were not to leave the country without risk. The news of their presence was telegraphed from town to town; motor-cars mounting machine guns and anti-aircraft cannon were dispatched at full speed to the most likely points; observers were specially detailed to watch the Swiss border and to note whether these adventurers crossed the frontier. But such was the extraordinary speed with which the airmen returned, that scarcely had the news of their arrival been received than the airmen themselves were over the place to which communication had been made and were out of sight before any effective step could be taken to intercept them.

The two officers, Lieutenant Sippe and Lieutenant Babington, were flying within sight of one another and at such a height that when they did come within the sphere of German anti-aircraft guns they defied every effort of the enemy to bring them down.

On the great barrack square of Belfort the French Commander waited anxiously as hours passed without news coming to him of the result of the raid. Situated as Belfort is, so close to the German frontier, it was impossible that the French should gain any news of the absent airmen from any distance, and the first intimation that the General and his Staff received was the sudden appearance in the air of two swooping aeroplanes which dived down on to the square and came to a halt within a few paces of where the Staff was waiting.

For this service the three officers, including Commander Briggs, were awarded the Legion of Honour by the French Government.

At Düsseldorf and Cologne it might reasonably have been supposed that the enemy was immune from attack, that they lay too far within their own borders to be subjected to the indignity of a bombardment at this stage of the war. Friedrichshafen, still farther away from the French frontier, never imagined that so outrageous a thing would happen as an attack upon its Zeppelin shed. But if there were two places which apparently were more secure than any other from attack either by land or sea, they were Wilhelmshaven and Cuxhaven. These, indeed, might be called the very sanctuary of Prussian naval life.

With waters protected by minefields thickly sown, with batteries placed at every point which commanded the approach of the Elbe, with Zeppelin bases left and right, and the whole of the German Navy anchored within reach of the Kiel Canal, the defences were so strong it would need more than an ordinarily desperate adventurer to place his head in the lion's mouth.

An air raid upon Cuxhaven was never seriously thought of by the German naval and military authorities, and no adequate provision was made to fight off such a raider. What was very clear to the German was that the nearest hostile land was separated by some 350 miles of water and that a raider would necessarily be compelled to make a 700 mile journey in the air. As it proved, such a journey was not necessary.

On Christmas Eve, Undaunted and Arethusa, attended by a small flotilla of fast torpedo boat destroyers, moved out of one of our ports and made their way across the North Sea. Piled high on the decks of these little cruisers, the newest and some of the most efficient of Britain's ships, were seven water planes.

There are certain of His Majesty's ships which are specially equipped for carrying water-planes ready for launching. One of these is Hibernia. Certainly neither Undaunted nor Arethusa were so equipped, and a strange sight they must have presented as they moved across the heaving waters with their strange cargoes. Their objective was a point not many miles south of Heligoland. It was no sudden raid against an undefended coast line, no hurried bombardment that this fleet had in view, a bombardment of a few minutes followed by a precipitous flight to safety, but a calm and leisured attack upon the very heart of the German naval service.

That they were sighted almost instantly is evident.

The Zeppelins on the island were first brought into action. They came looming from their great sheds, and rose upward, moving over the waters, already alive with submarine craft. The British captains knew their danger; they also knew the limitations of the enemy's submarines.

They must remain at a distance which would enable them to operate without fear of being struck by the British shells. Even here they were in some danger if they so much as put their periscope above water. They had, however, torpedoes, and these they launched against the daring raiders. The fast ships, such as Undaunted and Arethusa, had little to fear from torpedo attacks, so long as they knew the quarter from which that attack would be launched. The torpedo in its course through the sea leaves a distinct track, and the turn of a wheel will enable a fast moving cruiser to sweep clear from its path. Even against aircraft the dirigibles were ineffective, for here their uselessness was also clearly demonstrated. Three shells from the Undaunted driven straight into the air and bursting in alarming proximity to one great gasbag, set it swirling about, and another three sent up from the Arethusa completed the rout. The enemy's aeroplanes managed to get somewhere over the cruisers—a position in which it was impossible to shell them—and dropped several bombs, none of which, however, found its mark.

For three hours this extraordinary combat went on—a fight between a little sea-going fleet and the unseen peril which lurked in the ocean's depths, and the whirling terror which circled far above the cruisers.

In the meantime the British airmen had gone straight to their objective, which was Cuxhaven. Rising to almost the maximum height, they were enabled not only to see the little town for which they were making, but also to gain a fairly clear view of the whole of the Kiel Canal and the Shilig roadstead, wherein a portion of the German Fleet lay at anchor. Instantly every gun in the vicinity was trained upon these seven specks, but without result. Spreading farther and farther apart, each man taking one particular section for reconnaissance, the airmen covered the ground allotted to them. Two detached themselves and flew direct for Cuxhaven, dropping bombs on their way upon the warships and making at least one hit.

The pilots engaged in this raid were Flight-Commander Douglas Oliver, R.N., Flight-Commander Francis Hewlett, R.N., Flight-Commander Robert Ross, R.N., Flight-Commander Cecil Kilner, R.N., Flight-Commander Arnold Miley, R.N., Flight-Lieutenant Charles Edmonds, R.N., Flight-Sub-Lieutenant Vivian Gaskell Blackburn, R.N. Of these all but one succeeded in returning to the vicinity of Undaunted and Arethusa in the place where they had been left and whence they had driven back all hostile attacks.

CHAPTER VI — TURKEY AND THE DARDANELLES

The German's object in scheming to include Turkey in the war is plainly to be seen. He hoped to produce a revolution in Egypt, and he had good reasons for his hope, for the Khedive had evidently been in his pay and had been acting in concert with the enemies of Britain. He hoped, by directing the Turk to an invasion of Egypt, to hold a portion of the British Army along the Suez Canal, and by an offensive towards the Caucasus to employ a considerable number of Russian troops to the relief of his sorely tried neighbour. More than this, he hoped that the deflection of one who termed himself "The Commander of the Faithful," would have the effect of stirring Mussulman opinion in India, and creating that condition of anarchy which it was the fond conviction of the great German General Staff would follow the Sultan's act.

She possessed two old German battleships, one of which, after the declaration of war, was employed to guard the mine fields which the Turk had so plentifully sown in the Dardanelles.

Though old, she had good fighting value, and Lieutenant Holbrook, commanding the submarine B11 (the Mediterranean Fleet was never far from the entrance of the Dardanelles) thought her of sufficient importance to venture on a most perilous undertaking. Messudiyeh, old as she was, represented the best part of Turkey's battleship fleet. This large ship was Lieutenant Holbrook's objective, but it could only be secured after a long voyage and by the safe negotiation of these deadly mine barriers. Nothing daunted, the little submarine started off on its extraordinary voyage. Sinking almost to the bed of the sea, it worked a cautious way forward against treacherous currents, and dodged no fewer than five rows of mines by diving under them. In this manner the B11 was able to come upon the unsuspecting Messudiyeh before the crew of the vessel were alive to their peril. Even as they recognised their danger, the torpedo was loosed to its deadly work, and in a flash of flame and a shock of explosion which set the submarine rolling like a row-boat in a storm, this ancient battleship went out. For this daring deed Lieutenant Holbrook was awarded the V.C. He succeeded in getting safely back, although assailed by gun- fire and torpedo boats, having been submerged on one occasion for as long a period as nine hours.

The Dardanelles from the Mediterranean, to where its waters broaden out into the Sea of Marmora, is roughly forty miles in length, allowing for its tortuous windings; as the crow flies the distance might be reduced to about thirty miles. The Straits vary in width from nearly five miles to about three-quarters of a mile.

The big enterprise of attempting to force the Dardanelles had been kept a great secret, and the first news came as a surprise to most people. It was to be a fight of big naval guns against land forts. There were many who held that the advantage lay with the latter. The stupendous nature of the undertaking may be realised by the fact that forty or more ships were employed to prosecute the work.

If we in Great Britain were ignorant of what was going forward in that quarter of the globe, the people of the Levant talked of nothing else. It was there the most open of secrets that the Fleets were assembling for an attack upon the guarded passage which cuts the Turkish Empire from the rest of Europe. The sinking of Scharnhorst, Gneisenau, Nürnberg, and Leipzig by Admiral Sturdee's fleet had left the seas untroubled by the enemy, save for a couple of light cruisers and a converted liner, all of which were subsequently accounted for. To hunt these sufficient ships were detailed, but the battleships and battle cruisers were ordered back into the Mediterranean for a new adventure. An attempt had already been made in November, when a combined squadron of French and British ships had commenced a bombardment of the outer forts at a range of seven miles. This bombardment only lasted for a very short time. The fleets were taking sighting shots, and, whatever was the result of that preliminary bombardment, evidently there was encouragement to be found, as was to be proved three months later.

Possibly it was with a sigh of relief that the Turk watched the small British and French squadron disappear over the horizon after their little bombardment on that occasion; he might reasonably suppose, as days passed into weeks and weeks into months without any return of his tormentor, that his enemy had accepted as gospel the traditions which hung about the impregnability of land fortifications. But the lapse of time was only being employed by the British and the French to make good their preparations. The laden supply ships came into Malta, fleets were carefully organised and the practice of crews was specially directed to the great task which all knew was ahead.

The fruition of all these preparations was seen on February 19th, when the Allied fleet which had been assembled for the great task, appeared before the entrance of the Dardanelles, and, without any preliminary or further preparation, began a bombardment of the great forts which cover the entrance to the Straits. These, the one situated on the Gallipoli Peninsula and the other on the

Asiatic side of the Straits, were respectively Seddul Bahr and Kum Kale. At eight o'clock in the morning the first ship opened fire, and throughout the day the bombardment was continued until three in the afternoon, when observers had noticed the destruction which had been wrought amongst the heavy guns. Then it was that the fleet closed in and, at remarkably short range, began to pour a rain of shell into the doomed forts. By evening one fort on the Asiatic side alone was firing; the remainder of the forts were silent.

In these operations some of the ships engaged, under Vice-Admiral Sackville H. Carden, were Vengeance, Cornwallis, Triumph, Suffren, Gaulois, Bouvet, Inflexible, and Agamemnon.
The entrance forts which, like their fellows, were armed with Krupp guns, represented indeed a serious obstacle to any attempt which might be made to force the Straits. Isolated forts, notably at Dardanus, half-way between the entrance and the Narrows on the Asiatic side, and Kephez Point, a little to the north of that town, with a number of earthworks at intervals on the Gallipoli Peninsula, rendered any attempt at hasty progression a very dangerous undertaking. Apart from the groups at the entrance, there was a very strong group at Chanak, which included the main Chanak battery, the Parkeh and Pehemenni batteries; whilst on the opposite shore at Kilid Bahr ("the gate of the sea") were other strong works.

The immediate continuance of the bombardment was interrupted by the condition of bad weather. Mist, a low visibility, and a strong south-westerly gale rendered operations extremely difficult. On February 25 the bombardment was resumed, and all the forts at the entrance were successfully reduced.

It was not until February 28 that the Admiralty made an important announcement. The condensed and laconic reports which had been issued from Naval Headquarters gave us an indication that besides the ships which had been mentioned there was one which possessed a much more powerful armament than the others. This was revealed as the Queen Elizabeth, our newest super-Dreadnought, armed with eight 15-inch guns. Never before had such a powerful warship come into action, and her arrival on the scene marked a new era, not only in the local operations, but in the history of naval warfare.

It had been Queen Elizabeth, Agamemnon, Irresistible, and Gaulois which had reduced the fort at Cape Helles at long range. As giving the lie to the Turkish assertion that the guns at the entrance were obsolete weapons, we have the fact that the fort at Cape Helles, replying to the fire at 11,000 yards, hit Agamemnon, killing three men and seriously wounding five.

The mine-sweepers had therefore little to fear from the outer forts; but, leaving nothing to chance, the destroyers, supported by a battleship, followed slowly into the entrance of the Straits and covered the sweeping for a distance of four miles.

Immediately following the reduction of the forts at the entrance, a large force of marines and sailors had been put ashore to clear away any straggling troops which might be found in that neighbourhood, and also to render what aid could be given to the Turkish wounded. A brisk little fight with a much stronger force than had been anticipated produced a few British casualties, but the marines established themselves at the edge of the battered forts and were for some time able to hold their own, though eventually they were obliged to withdraw.

The importance of the first operations against the Dardanelles cannot be over- estimated. The bitterest criticism was levelled against those who undertook the task of attempting to force the Straits without the aid of an army to engage the rapidly increasing land forces of Turkey, but it is certain that with all its errors of judgment, the operations were justified and for a time it looked as though we should succeed by gunfire alone in reducing the guardian fortresses. Politically the attempt produced sensational results. It galvanised the neutral nations of the Balkans to life and alarm. It precipitated a crisis in Greece and created something like panic in Constantinople. Bulgaria's position, Roumania's position, and the very future of the Austro- Hungarian Empire depended upon the ability of Turkey to keep at bay the battering warships. And there was another reason for this bombardment, which was even more vital to the Allies than the question of the continuance of Bulgaria and Roumania's neutrality, and that was the very urgent need which existed for opening a way into Russia.

Exactly what Great Britain was called upon to provide, in the shape of armaments and supplies for the Allied nations, we were not told at the moment; but it is certain that a free interchange, not only of trade in war materials but in commerce, was absolutely necessary. Russia's one port, Archangel, is from the end of November till the beginning of May icebound, and Russia must depend entirely upon the stock of ammunition, motor-cars, etc., which she stored up before the ice set, and which with the Dardanelles closed she had no hope of replenishing.

CHAPTER VII — THE LAND OPERATIONS

The high hopes we entertained of a successful offensive from the sea were doomed to remain unfulfilled. The German-Turkish defences included mobile shore batteries which played havoc with the mine-sweepers, whilst drift-mines destroyed two British and one French warship, the latter, Bouvet, going down with practically all her crew.

It was after this tragedy that it was made abundantly clear to the British and the French Governments that a new plan of campaign must be adopted in the Dardanelles. The naval plan itself was excellent. It had silenced a large number of forts, but had actually reduced only a very few. For your Turkish gunner, flinching under the heavy hail of shell which the battleships concentrated upon the fortresses, would disappear to his bomb-proof shelter and wait until the storm passed over. And the guns of that fort would to all intents and purposes be "silenced."

From a distance the naval gunners could not be certain that they had succeeded in their object, but could not afford to take the risk of believing that they had failed. The ammunition supply for big guns was not an unlimited one, and no captain would continue his bombardment of a fort which had ceased to reply. He might keep his eye upon that fort for the remainder of the day, and at the first sign of activity renew his attack. But if hour passed hour and no sign of life was seen, he must, for economy's sake, regard the silencing as being permanent.

And the next morning, when the Fleet again returned to the Dardanelles to continue the work, he would be pardonably exasperated to discover himself under the direct fire of the guns which he imagined to be destroyed. Only by the landing of demolishing parties could the Naval authorities be absolutely certain that the power for mischief had been broken.

Moreover, there was another source of embarrassment to the attacking fleet. Mine-sweepers, going forward to trawl the minefields, were subjected to heavy fire directed on them from unsuspected positions on both shores. Protecting battleships might reply; aviators might accurately locate the places where the guns were concealed—though this was a much more difficult task than many people imagined—and the offending battery might be put hors de combat, only to discover that another battery, which all this time had lain quiescent and unnoticed, opened as heavy a bombardment upon the trawlers the moment they pushed forward to their work.

Obviously, therefore, the shore had to be cleared. A line of troops must slowly and thoroughly sweep the Peninsula, finishing the work which the naval guns had begun, destroying concealed torpedo stations, and making it impossible for the Turkish Army to hamper or embarrass the Allied Navy in its work. For this purpose, two armies of considerable size were organised on the north coast of Africa. The first of these was largely composed of Regular, Territorial, and British Colonial troops, and a very fine army, considerably strengthened by artillery from France and consisting of French Colonials and French first line soldiers, under the command of General d'Amade. The whole expedition was commanded by General Sir Ian Hamilton, an officer who had rendered excellent service in the South African war, and was at the outbreak of hostilities organising the Imperial forces overseas.

During the months of February and March and the greater part of April, the preparations went on; plans were made, the naval and military authorities combining; fleets of transports came laden to certain of the Mediterranean stations; and whilst the warships continued their long-range bombardment of the Turkish forts, the Allies organised their efforts to seize and hold the Gallipoli Peninsula.

That preparation coincided with an extraordinary effort on the part of the Turk. He did not intend to waste the time the partial inactivity of his enemy afforded him. Troops came down from Constantinople, the best fighting men were withdrawn from Syria; new field artillery and howitzer batteries were brought along to Gallipoli; and Turkish engineers, under German direction, began to make the most elaborate and thorough preparations to meet the threatened attack.

The Gallipoli Peninsula is a tongue of land which runs south-westward and follows the rough shape which is peculiar to many such geographical formations which are washed by a westerly sea. (Of these, the best known are the "toe" of Italy and the County of Cornwall.) It is separated from the Asiatic shore by a stretch of water which for thirty miles is known as the Straits of Dardanelles, connecting the Aegean Sea with the Sea of Marmora. From the entrance of the Straits, at Seddul Bahr to Gallipoli, there is never more than a four-mile width of water between the Peninsula and the Asiatic shore, and at a certain point, some ten miles from Seddul Bahr, the Straits are pinched so that there is less than a mile between shore and shore. These are the famous Narrows, and are heavily protected by terraces of forts.

The Peninsula itself is a somewhat confused and hilly country; the hills are not of any great eminence, 650 feet being the supreme height of the majority, though the range which dominates the westerly side of the Peninsula is considerably higher. Between these hills run a number of roads which are little more than sand tracks, and in the folds of the hills are to be found a few squalid and unimportant villages, mostly inhabited by an agricultural population. On the coast, and particularly facing the Straits there are a number of well-to-do communities and villages which might be dignified by the name of towns, and of these, Maidos, above the Narrows, Chanak, on the Narrows themselves, and Dardenos, further towards the sea, are the most important. Beyond Maidos is Gallipoli, which is the first of the big towns seen by the visitor to Constantinople who negotiates the Dardanelles.

The beaches where any landing could take place were necessarily few in a country presenting the topographical features of the Peninsula. The Asiatic shore would have been a much simpler problem, but obviously the main advance must be toward the enemy's capital and toward the enemy's strength, and this would have to be on the European side.

The Turk's preparations were very thorough, and on the hills commanding all the beaches he established, under German direction, strong and formidable defences. Guns were placed so cunningly that even the ubiquitous British airman might not be able to locate them. Nearer to the beach, in positions as commanding, batteries of machine-guns, Maxims and improved gatlings were placed to cover the various beaches, whilst the ruins of forts and villages which had been destroyed by shell-fire from the British ships were also set in order for defence.

Von der Goltz, the German charged with the defence of the Dardanelles, made a rapid tour of the defences and found them good. "If the British land here," telegraphed one of his correspondents to a Berlin paper, "it will be wonderful. If, when they land, they force the Turkish defences, it will be a miracle. The British are beaten before they begin."

The great difficulties of the task were not under-estimated by the commanders of the Allied forces. "This is not a question of 'If at first you don't succeed, try, try again'," wrote the official correspondent, "because unless enormous reinforcements can be spared from the Western theatre of war, Constantinople will have to be taken from the Black Sea by a Russian army landing in Thrace. We shall have to admit that we undertook a task that was beyond our powers with the forces available, and leave it to others, or only strike again when the Russians can cooperate at the Bosphorus. But, judged from any standpoint, the task involves enormous difficulties.

"We have to land an army in the face of an enemy who has had ample warning that he may expect such an attempt. We have to put on shore food, water, guns, horses, munitions, ammunition, and all the thousand odd things necessary to keep an army in the field, besides making arrangements to remove a large number of wounded and sick. In this we are very largely dependent on the state of the weather, which, if it continues capricious, may leave one part of our army ashore, whilst the remainder and the supplies are held off the coast by a rough sea. Again, an army which has perforce been kept on transports for a long period cannot have the manoeuvring efficiency of an army which has been trained and handled by its generals on land. The command will also be a very difficult one to exercise, and will depend largely on the efficiency of the leaders of brigades, as when the Army is finally ashore at various points, widely separated, the Headquarters Staff will only be able to exercise a very general control.

"I do not believe we can hope to surprise the Turks, led as they are by German officers, by the sudden arrival of this huge force off the shores of Gallipoli. We may effect a local night surprise, and that is all. You cannot keep the news of the assembly of a huge expedition such as this from leaking out in the East. The news of the concentration of this mass of warships and transports in Mudros Bay has undoubtedly found its way by a hundred different channels to Constantinople.

"Neither can we overlook the fact that the enemy is fighting for his very existence, and will therefore bring every available man and gun into the field. The moment the first British ship is past the Narrows, the Turkish Empire in Europe has ceased to exist. No one knows this better than the Turks themselves. Had they their own way they would probably prefer to make an eleventh-hour peace rather than put this tremendous issue, affecting as it does their very existence as an independent nation, to the test.

"But they know they have gone too far, and can only expect terms which would leave them very little better off than if they lose all by fighting. Therefore they must fight and stand or fall by the result. They are in a desperate position, and may be expected to fight like desperate men."

On Saturday night, April 24th, the Turkish watchers in various posts of observation saw, steaming slowly across the sea, a fleet of a size greater than had ever been seen in these waters—crowds of torpedo craft, grey, formidable cruisers, and behind these, battleship after battleship in array. Then came the transports—liners of every conceivable size and shape, big passenger boats, colliers and smaller craft. "They lined the horizon," said an observer, and he did not exaggerate. The transports lay at a considerable distance from the shore.

In the dark of the night, with all lights extinguished, the big fleet began to creep in shore. All the previous Sunday the heavier guns of the fleet had been shelling the forts of the Straits and searching the known lines of Turkish entrenchments. "We found craters into which you could have put a house," said a naval officer, "but the Turkish trenches and their gun positions were so well made that it is doubtful if any great damage was done in the preliminary bombardment."

The method of landing may be briefly described. In the early hours of the morning, certain of the warships, carrying large covering parties of troops, moved as closely in shore as possible, and sent off a number of boats, towed by a steam pinnace, toward the beach. Each line of boats will be referred to in this chapter as "a tow," and tows were taken not only by the small steam-boats of the fleet but by the destroyers, and in one case by a submarine. The task of the first landing force was to secure a foothold upon the beaches and cover the landing of the greater army when that foothold had been made good.

First let us follow the fortunes of the Australians and New Zealanders, whose task it was to seize and hold the country about Gaba Tepe. This is a point half- way up the western coast of the Peninsula. The landing was carried out at dawn, under a heavy and enfilading fire. Here, as at other places, a strip of beach leads to an almost perpendicular "bluff," and the position has been best described, and will be best understood by those who know the place, as bearing a remarkable resemblance to the Leas at Folkestone. The abruptness of the bluff to a large extent saved the Australians and New Zealanders from greater punishment than they might otherwise have received. Under the shelter of the cliffs they were able to consolidate their position.

Enfiladed left and right by gun fire, the whole beach swept by shrapnel, the Australians and New Zealanders began their ascent of the cliff, and did not waver. Left and right, seeking for whatever foothold they could, these gallant men from overseas progressed, with a steadiness under fire which merited the praise of all who witnessed the manoeuvre. Rallied at the edge of the cliff, they drove home a bayonet attack which swept the Turk from his advanced position, and such was their impetuosity that many of them penetrated farther inland than was desired, and suffered heavily in a counter-attack delivered by the Turk in full strength.

A long ridge, terminating to the north in Coja Chemin, a mountain rising to nearly 1,000 feet was their objective. But their immediate business was to afford cover for the landing of bigger forces, to push out their front so that those who came after might be free from attack by rifle and machine gun; and this they did effectively. Though the enemy might drop a curtain of shrapnel between shore and transports—as he did—the new troops disembarked rapidly and in comparative immunity, and any fear that the landing would fail was dissipated.

The ten-mile stretch of rocky foreshore to the west of the Gallipoli Peninsula presented an extraordinary sight upon this Sunday morning. The transports loomed through the mist, the raging, hammering battleships plastered the disputed cliffs and hills with shrapnel and high explosives, the rattle of musketry came from the shore as the khaki specks moved slowly forward and upward. On this ten-mile line the fight proceeded furiously. Sometimes, above the familiar detonation would come a deeper note. From somewhere behind the Peninsula a great shell would shriek, and pass generally to fall harmlessly between shore and battleship. There can be little doubt that this unknown ship, which fired at such a remarkable range, and which very often came dangerously near to hitting its mark, was the Goeben, whose arrival in Turkish waters had precipitated the war. Sometimes, and on various sectors of the coast, a new shell would explode against an enemy's position—a shell greater than any, spurting fountains of earth and stones. This indicated the presence and the watchful care of the Queen Elizabeth.

Whilst the fighting was going on at Gaba Tepe, things were going forward elsewhere. The difficult business of landing was proceeding at the southern, end of the Peninsula. There were roughly five beaches chosen for landing the Expeditionary Force. The first two of these were to the north of Cape Tekeh, on the westerly side of the Peninsula. The third was immediately between Cape Tekeh and Cape Helles. The fourth was between Cape Helles and Seddul Bahr; and the fifth in Morto Bay. If you were to superimpose upon the map of the Peninsula a clock face, just as when one is endeavouring to train the young idea in shooting one imagines the target a clock and teaches him the hours at which he is to aim; and if, on this clock face, you make "eleven" represent the place of the northerly landing, ten as the next, eight as the next, between six and seven the fourth, and four o'clock the fifth, you have a rough idea as to the locality of the places which were chosen. Perhaps it will lead to a better understanding of what occurred if we follow the example of the official correspondent, and, taking beach by beach from left to right, recount the doings of that fateful April 25th.

Those who know the Peninsula will know that the foreshore is of an extremely rocky character, broken here and thereby broad stretches of beach, behind which are either fairly even valleys, partly under cultivation, or else that tangle of little hills to which I have already made reference. On the northerly beach, that is to say, that which was nearest to the Australians and New Zealanders, H.M.S. Dublin, Amethyst and Sapphire covered the landing of two battalions and one company, and here the troops reached terra firma without encountering any very solid opposition. We will call this No. I landing, and it accounted itself fortunate, for it was very evident that both No. 2 and No. 3, farther down, and especially No. 3, were having a very bad time. Encouraged by the easiness of their success, the two battalions moved forward inland through a stiff and difficult country, and it seemed that the task, which had been so long and so persistently discussed and about which all sorts of speculations had been rife, was by no means as difficult as had been anticipated.

Yet, as a matter of fact, the landing of No. 1 party was doomed to be the only landing which was a failure. Very soon the advancing infantry came in touch with the enemy.

It must be remembered that, save for a few very light guns, the landing had been wholly unsupported by those arms which are successful to an advance of infantry. Before this little force there gathered regiment after regiment of Turkish infantry.

Disputing every foot of the way, No. 1 force fell slowly back to the cliff, where it held on grimly through the night. Its commanders had discovered beyond doubt that progress in this region was impossible, and on the Monday morning, covered by the gun fire of the protecting cruisers, the force was re-embarked. Therefore, in respect to this party, the Turkish claim that they "had driven the English to the sea" was justified.

Whilst they had been battling their way forward, No. 2 force, a mile or so to the south, had made the most successful landing of the day. The Implacable, which conveyed the troops, stood in to the shore, its quartermasters in the chains sounding the depth until she had reached six fathoms. Farther off, the Swiftsure engaged herself in a bombardment, which was supported by the Implacable. The great 12-inch guns of the battle cruiser swept the higher ground with shrapnel, whilst its smaller armaments kept up an incessant fire along the beach and beyond.

Here again, the troops found a low cliff which, being scaled, revealed a plateau of practically level ground for two miles. The Implacable kept up her hammering at the furthermost Turkish defences, and the troops, moving rapidly to the shore, formed up and began their advance. Soon they were met with the inevitable fire at a thousand yards, and entrenched themselves. Later in the day they delivered a heavy counter-attack but were forced back.

Farther south, No. 3 party was in difficulties, and though No. 2 extended its right, and to some extent rendered service to its less fortunate comrades, it was necessary for the second party again to entrench itself. The more necessary was this because from the Krithia plateau, to the northeast, the enemy brought his guns into action, one especially proving most troublesome until the busy Implacable turned its attention upon the attacker and, after a few shots, succeeded in finding the gun position.

Part of the Turkish force which had driven off No. 1 was now sweeping forward in Echelon to No. 2, and this gallant little force fell back to the cliff, holding on grimly through the night. On the Monday morning the situation had developed farther south, and they were able to advance.

No. 3 landing was between Tekeh and Helles, and here was a scene of terrible fighting and of casualties heavier than were sustained either in the Australians' landing, in the abortive landing of No. 1 party, or that more successful effort which was made by No. 2 on its right. The beach chosen was that across which the Turk had believed the main effort of his enemy would be made. To the left Cape Tekeh rose, 30 metres high; to the right Cape Helles; and in the centre the broad beach, defended by triple lines of barbed-wire entrenchments, by trenches cleverly concealed, and by a whole host of snipers who, from the cover which the rough country afforded, were able to pick off the men as they came to land. There were eight "tows." Four of these moved toward Cape Helles and gained the cover of the cliff; two toward Cape Tekeh, and two made for the gentle landing which the beach afforded.

Euryalus, which had made the tows, kept up a furious fire upon the enemy's position, but in the centre, covering this beach, the Turk was so well placed and so widely spread that it was impossible for the ship to offer any assistance. Long before the two tows reached the shore, bullets were falling thickly in the crowded boats, or splashing in the water about.

Machine-gun and pom-pom sent a whizzing hail of death to the invaders, and under that withering fire nothing could live. Every man of the ill-fated party which attempted to make the landing on the beach was stricken down.

The larger force to the right, which gained the shelter of Cape Helles, was more successful. Covered to an extent by the cliff and by the trenches which they hastily constructed, the men endeavoured desperately to retrieve the fortunes of the centre; but they were firing at an unseen enemy, as well protected from rifles as he was from guns. There was nothing to do for this unit of the 29th Division but to begin an ascent of the cliff and endeavour to work round the enemy in the centre. Simultaneously, the men from the remaining tows scrambled up the cliff, and hung on with "tooth and claw" through the morning, raked by shrapnel, a target for innumerable snipers, and bearing unflinchingly the concentrated fire of masked machine-gun batteries.

At ten o'clock in the morning (Sunday, the 24th), another battalion was landed at No. 3, and moved to the left to get in touch with No. 2; but all thought of offensive was checked at nightfall, and the full power of British endurance was tested to resist a terrible assault which was delivered by an enemy outnumbering the British six to one. For a moment the battle line swayed dangerously. Men fought in the darkness with bayonets and with entrenching tools. Trenches were carried by sheer weight of numbers, and regained by the indomitable courage of the defenders. Lit by star shells and the momentary flash of bursting shrapnel, the scene was terrible to contemplate. Line after line of red-fezzed Turks, marching shoulder to shoulder according to the best German military tradition, came charging forward against the scanty single line of trenches which the British held.

On the beach below—the battle occurred on the higher ground—were beach parties who were bringing ashore munitions and provisions for the army. They consisted of men of the Navy, Engineers and staff officers, and when the fight was at its most critical point the order came for the beach parties to seize their rifles, come up to the firing line and assist as best they could to reject the cumulative push of the Turk to dislodge the gallant regiments from their foothold. In the darkness some of the beach parties were unable to find their rifles, but, seizing whatever weapon was nearest—an axe, a spade or a pick handle—they scrambled up the hill and joined their comrades in the trenches.

All the deeds of heroism which were performed that night will never be known. One midshipman who had charged himself with the duty of keeping a certain section of the trench supplied with ammunition, came toiling painfully up the hill with a dozen bandoliers of ammunition hung about him. He was struck full in the chest and knocked over by a bullet, but rose again and continued his journey. Again he was struck and again he fell, and rose. Yet a third time did an enemy bullet find him. Nevertheless, he delivered his supply of ammunition to the trenches, each bullet having been struck against and been diverted by one of the cartridges in a bandolier.

Throughout the night the fight raged, and the morning sun saw our men, weary- eyed but triumphant, holding the trench from which the legions of Turkey had failed to drive them. Whilst the landing was going on under these terrible conditions, No. 4 party were engaged in what was the most novel and at the same time one of the most punishing operations which the landing saw. No. 4 undoubtedly suffered more casualties than any other force, and had to meet with an opposition even greater than that which faced No. 3. No. 3, it will be remembered, was landed between Cape Tekeh and Cape Helles. No. 4's landing place was between Cape Helles and Seddul Bahr. To the right was the ruined fortress which had borne this name, and which had been first of all silenced by the guns of the fleet, and afterwards demolished by landing parties. Nevertheless the wreckage offered splendid cover for infantry. The town of Seddul Bahr was a ruin, yet its walls, its rubble heaps, and the towers of the forts which still stood made excellent cover for an enemy who, it must be admitted, braving all the dangers which bombardment threatened, manned the towers with their machine-guns, and threw out trenches near to the beach to oppose the landing.

Topographically, the situation was rather similar to that which had met No. 3 party. There was the same broad stretch of beach, the same flanking hills, the same broken country beyond, and in addition the excellent cover which Seddul Bahr itself afforded.

Sir Ian Hamilton had realised that the fight here would be the fiercest and the approach to the beach the most dangerous.

He had provided a liner, the River Clyde, and she had been made ready for the purpose to which she was eventually put.

Great exits had been cut in her sides and over her bows; her bridge had been covered with steel plates, and here twelve Maxim guns, well shielded, had been installed. From the gangways cut in her side planks had been suspended, and it was the intention to run the ship aground upon the shelving beach, drop over the gangways, and allow the soldiers who were confined in the shelter of her steel sides to rush the beach and its defences.

Behind the beach, and filling up the gap between Cape Helles and Seddul Bahr, was a hill which is known as 141, heavily entrenched and protected by barbed- wire entanglements. As the ship approached the shore and her intentions became obvious, a fire not only from Cape Helles to the left, from the fortifications on the right, but from the almost impregnable position ahead, was opened upon the River Clyde.

The transport was preceded by eight tows, but the River Clyde must have overtaken these as they grounded simultaneously. The object of the tows was to gain the cover of the rising ground and such shelter as the cliffs to left and right of the position afforded. The River Clyde was to provide a large force, some 2,000 men in all, to carry the enemy positions by a frontal attack and to make good the ground for further landings. The task set this force, when contemplated in cold blood, seems impossible.

Not only were they enfiladed from positions strongly fortified, not only was the sand full of pitfalls and covered thickly by barbed-wire, from behind which the entrenched snipers could pick off the landing party at their leisure; but there was in the rear the impregnable position of Hill 141.

There can have been no more extraordinary sight in the war than that which was presented by the River Clyde, as, going full speed ahead, her huge bows casting the shallow waters aside in two waves, she headed straight for the land. Her bridge was aflame with Maxim fire. Wherever a machine-gun could be placed, it was so placed. Yet, although she carried two battalions aboard, "packed like sardines" there was no sign of any human being at whom the enemy might direct their aim.

Pom-pom shells and Maxim bullets rattled on the steel shell of the ship like the beats of a kettledrum. Only the protection which her steel skin gave to them prevented her occupants from being wiped out. Presently her keel caught the bottom, and she heaved up and came to a standstill, her screws still revolving furiously. She was still too far off the shore to enable her to get her troops landed. This contingency had been provided for. A hopper which had followed directly in her wake came alongside and drove ahead.

A lighter was hauled round and the gangway lowered. Volunteers were called for to make the first landing, and although they knew they were going to certain death, the two hundred nearest the gangway clamoured for permission.

The shots were falling like tropical rain as that intrepid two hundred flew across the gangway plank, sprang over the uneven decks of the lighter and dropped on to the sand. Some were shot almost before they had left the ship's protection; others were swept from the gangway; some reached the lighter; and a very few—and those desperately wounded—managed to reach the shore and to crawl under the protection of a high bank of sand near the water's edge.

The attempt had failed. It was madness to send other men the same way, and the officer commanding the troops ordered the "stand-fast." Within the cover of the ship they were safe, and although, we may be sure, they grumbled at the reaction, the men settled down with admirable philosophy to what proved a day- long wait.

This failure had been signalled back to the fleet, and the battleships Cornwallis, Albion, and Queen Elizabeth opened a furious bombardment upon the enemy's position, a bombardment with secondary armaments and with 12 and 15- inch guns, which did not cease for hours on end. The position was an extraordinarily exposed one, and the Turks were not slow to realise how excellent a mark the stranded ship might be. The word was telegraphed across to the Turkish gun positions on the Asiatic shore, and howitzers immediately opened fire upon the stranded vessel. Quick as this happened, every ship in sight turned its attention upon this luckless howitzer battery. Four times the River Clyde was struck by shells, without, however, any great damage being occasioned; and then the crescendo of fire from the vengeful warships turned the enemy howitzer to scrap iron, and no more danger was experienced from that quarter.

In the afternoon the men of No. 3, who had effected a landing, moved to the right, and probably got in touch with those of No. 4 who had secured a foothold at Cape Helles. Displaying the greatest gallantry, this little party carried one of the enemy's trenches at the point of the bayonet, but this did not affect the general position so far as the cramped men on the River Clyde were concerned. Then darkness fell, and at eight o'clock, when the enemy's fire had first slackened and then died away, the commander of the River Clyde decided to effect his landing. With extraordinary expedition the men got ashore without sustaining a single casualty.

This was the great surprise of the day.

The opposition had been so strenuous, and the determination of the Turk to prevent a landing in force here so apparent, that No. 4 might expect that the worst of the work lay ahead of them. So far as the landing was concerned, however, that worst did not materialise, and the party was able to entrench itself and prepare for the inevitable counter-attack before that counter-attack was launched.

The mystery of that lull, which enabled the British to make good their landing and to organise a defence, has not been explained. It was the one bad blunder which the Turk and the German committed. They seemed to come to a realisation of their folly at eleven o'clock, and an assault in force was delivered against the British positions, hand-to-hand fighting occurring all along the line. This attack was beaten off, but was followed by one even more serious, preparation being made for its delivery by a sustained and searching bombardment. The attack faded away toward the morning, but when dawn came and the little force was pushed forward, there was evidence that the enemy's resistance in this quarter was by no means finished.

Seddul Bahr was, as I have said, a mere jumble of mortar and bricks, of wrecked masonry, of shapeless masses of concrete and rusting guns. The pretty little town which lay beneath the fortress had long since been reduced to desolation by the guns of the fleet, and all that was left of forts and town consisted of a labyrinth of foundation walls, garden edges and rubble heaps. Unlovely a substitute as they made for the once picturesque village, they had a very definite military value, as we were to discover. Behind the open cellars and vaults, behind the brickwork and the scrambled masonry, was a veritable network of trenches, connecting up with Hill 141 on the front of the British position. Certain portions of the fort itself still stood, and had been well utilised by an ingenious enemy.

From one tower alone a dozen Maxims covered the British right; whilst from every stack of bricks, from every wall, and from such of the houses as had escaped demolition, came such a fire that the troops, seasoned as they had been in that short but grim battle of the night, flinched before it. It was only a momentary hesitation, and then the line poured forward into the first defences, bayoneted their occupants and crouched to the cover which their new ground afforded them.

The machine-guns in the tower were more than an ordinary handicap. It was obvious that no advance could be made until they were destroyed; and here again I would point out that these extraordinary accomplishments on the Gallipoli Peninsula were all carried out without the aid of field artillery and by comparatively small parties of men.

Back went the signal to the watchful warships laying off the Straits, and even as the machine-guns in the tower were rattling, the tower itself seemed to leap in the air in a cloud of smoke and flame, as two high explosive 12-inch shells struck it at one and the same time. It was the Cornwallis that was charged with the protection of the British right in this field, and excellently did she play her part. But now other ships were coming into action. The village had been won, the enemy driven from his walls and his emplacements, and Hill 141, with its immense entanglements, its earthen fortifications and its successive trench lines, invited the attention of the attacker.

By this time the men of No. 4 had been considerably reinforced, and before the attack began, Cornwallis, Queen Elizabeth and Albion opened a heavy fire upon the hills, searching crest and trench line and flinging their shrapnel against the protecting entanglements. At eleven o'clock on Monday morning, April 26th, the fourth force began its advance, and at 12 o'clock, after an hour of the fiercest fighting, where neither side gave nor asked for much quarter, the position was in their hands.

The fifth party had landed between Morto Bay and De Totts battery. This force consisted of 700 men, who were landed in trawlers, and though the fighting at this point was well contested, their adventures and the opposition which met them could not be compared with those which the third and the fourth had found.

In the meantime the French had landed at Kum Kale, on the Asiatic shore, and created a diversion, attracting to their front a much larger force than it was necessary the enemy should send. When their task had been accomplished they were re-embarked and brought across the mouth of the Straits and landed in the rear of the 700.

Summing up the position as the Commander-in-Chief found it on Monday morning, the 26th, the Australians and New Zealanders were holding firmly to the position they had established for themselves on the Sunday evening and during Sunday night. They had sustained heavy losses, a party having been cut off by the enemy, but they were holding a fairly unassailable post. Farther south, the British party No. 1, which had landed without opposition, had been driven back to the shore and been forced to re-embark. No. 2 was not only holding its position on the edge of the sea but was advancing. No. 3 had beaten off the main Turco-German attack, and now, considerably reinforced, was moving forward slowly but effectively. No. 4 had carried Seddul Bahr and Hill 141, and had pushed its line northward, joining up with No. 3 on its left and No. 5, which consisted of French and British troops, on its right.

It needed but a little further push to bring an intact British line right across the end of the Peninsula. On the night of the 26th there were few serious engagements, the exchanges being between snipers on the Australian front. The enemy had had such a hammering in this region that he could not immediately launch any further assault. Field guns had been landed, mounted batteries brought up to the front line, and many of the disadvantages under which the troops were suffering originally had been removed.

It was not only the actual work in the battle line that secured us our success. Behind the firing line and on the beaches the men of the Navy with their comrades of the Army were working day and night to land stores, water, munitions, guns, and horses for the guns, mules, ambulances. "Looking at the beach with its extraordinary litter of stores and material, it seemed as though there had been a great shipwreck and the equipment of a whole army washed up." On the beaches, too, temporary stores were being erected, bombproof shelters dug and roofed, depots established, and the despatch of supplies to the front line systematised.

The Navy had indeed accomplished tremendous work throughout the operations. A good idea of the diversity of the Navy's tasks in the Dardanelles was given us in the semi-official despatch.

"The whole of the responsibility for landing troops and keeping up the supplies of food and ammunition is in the Navy's hands, and in addition the responsibility of protecting the flanks of the combined armies and in keeping down the enemy's artillery fire lies with the warships. All troops, animals, guns, wagons, stores, ammunition, and a thousand other things have to be taken from the hundred transports lying off the Straits, which arrive full and leave empty for a fresh cargo at all hours of the day and night, and conveyed in trawlers or lighters to two narrow beaches, neither of which is more than 200 yards in width. The cliffs prohibit landing anything at any other point.

"Our naval commanders, lieutenants, and midshipmen in charge of this work have developed an efficiency which has astounded even the most tape-ridden theorists on how such matters should be carried through smoothly and with a minimum of delay. Piers have been built out into deep water by our sappers so that the largest lighters can come alongside. They have cut roads along the cliffs to increase the area of disembarkation, and a hundred devices have been introduced to lessen labour and increase efficiency, including systems of lighting which enable the work to go on uninterruptedly night and day. For it never stops, and even when the day's work is over and the last lighter has discharged her cargo, the streams of wounded are walking or being carried down to the beaches, where they are embarked on the empty barges and despatched for transportation to Egypt, to the hospital ships and transports.

"They keep watches on shore just as they do at sea, and their devotion to duty and keenness is just as marked as when facing the enemy's batteries in the Dardanelles. The line of demarcation between the authority of the Army and the Navy is strictly drawn. As long as a soldier, a horse, a gun, or a biscuit is on a ship, or on a lighter on its way to the shore, all are under the control of our beach parties.

"You see standing on one of the piers in the sweltering heat of the last few days, with the beach behind him crammed with men, stores, and animals, one of our young Kitcheners, with a megaphone in his hand, shouting orders to a dozen different lighters, each towed by a steam pinnace in the offing. One contains mules, another guns, a third biscuits, a fourth tinned meat, a fifth ammunition, a sixth troops, a seventh Generals and Staff officers. Everyone is directed to its right destination as if by some enchanter's wand, and no one dare step ashore until he has received his orders. At the end of the pier the naval authority ceases, and that of the Army begins.

"Here are Army Service Corps officers whose efficiency has become a by-word. All the hungry soldiers of our Allies or enemies are waiting to seize what the Navy has given them, and the thousand miscellaneous articles which look as if they never could be sorted are speedily divided, checked, and sent on their way down the lines of communication to the troops in the front trenches. The whole is a marvel of organisation. How it is managed will ever remain a mystery to me, but certainly such a task has never been attempted by an army and navy before. Neither let it be supposed that the work is carried out in peace and quiet. Far from it. The Turks on the Asiatic shore shell the beach almost every day.

"Our warships are continually engaged in trying to locate their guns and knock them out, or force them to change their positions. There is one gun, known as the 'Jewel of Asia,' which continually drops shells, but with a minimum of result. You hear the shriek of its arrival, then the explosion, followed by a cloud of sand out of which emerge figures of men and animals who should have been killed or injured, but who very seldom are."

By the night of the 27th, the Tuesday, after repulsing a Turkish attack which was delivered against the section of the line held by No. 2 party, the Allied force had established itself in an entrenched line running to a point about two miles to the north of Cape Tekeh, to a small plateau about De Totts battery, which had been occupied on the previous day by No. 5 party, at Eski Hissarlik, north of Morto Bay.

From April 28th until May 2nd there was a brief lull in the operations, but on the night of May 2nd a violent attempt by the enemy was made all along the line. It began at eight o'clock in the evening with a heavy and sustained bombardment, which did very little damage, though the range was excellent. To this we were now able to reply in kind. British field gun and French 75 gave shot for shot, whilst the howitzer batteries, which had been landed and brought up to the rear of the battle front with considerable difficulty, rendered valuable assistance. Immediately following the bombardment an assault in force was attempted, and division after division of Turkish infantry moved forward in dense formation to the task of breaking the British line. Our position was still parlous, for the superiority of force was with the enemy. A breach of the line, or anything which partook of the nature of defeat, could not fail to be disastrous.

Once let the Allies be beaten, and there could be no possible hope of retrievement. Behind them was the sea, and, powerful as were the guns of the Fleet, they could not possibly hope to save a broken army. As it happened, the attack ended disastrously for the enemy. Hundreds of machine-guns played upon the closely packed ranks, and the enemy was mown down by battalions. Giant searchlights, operated by men of the Navy, threw the reserves into prominence, and the 75-millimetre guns of the French artillery shattered and annihilated them. Following the destruction of these reserves the French infantry came into action and got in at close quarters with the bayonet, and the enemy retired, leaving his dead in heaps upon the ground.

The landing had been effected on April 26th, and a week of warfare had seen its line consolidated. Though the advance was no very great one, when reckoned by mileage, the achievement will stand for all time as one of the greatest military successes which the world has seen. The difficulties of the task were enormous, and even though the landing had been secured, it had been at a heavy cost. Before the entrenched line of the Allies were hills as strongly held and as completely guarded as any of those which they had taken. The Turkish Army had been reinforced from half-a-dozen different sources. Syria and Palestine had sent troops, originally intended for the invasion of Egypt; the garrisons at Adrianople had been denuded, and the Turks had even taken the hazardous step of withdrawing their garrisons from the frontiers of Greece, and this step was only arrested when the Greek Government of a sudden recalled M. Venizelos, the former Prime Minister, to confer with the Cabinet of Greece.

Before the troops that had effected their landing with such wonderful gallantry and at such heavy cost there now lay the height of Achi Baba to bar the progress of the Allies, and to possess the height, fortified with exceeding strength and cunning, was of necessity the next step in our deadly grapple with the Turk.

On May 6th new French and British regiments arrived on the scene, and the line which was holding the Turk in check was thickened. New and heavy artillery was landed, and both the French and our own Royal Field Artillery brought much needed reinforcements to support the Allied line.
All the beaches were now crowded with stores; wooden buildings had sprung up as if by magic, for the handy man had been busy night and day establishing base depots. A plentiful supply of water

had also been secured, and all the preliminary disadvantages under which our troops had laboured had disappeared. The shore parties still found trouble from the long range bombardment to which they were from time to time subjected, and landing held its spice of excitement from this cause. With the augmented forces General Sir Ian Hamilton began his serious attempt to reach the heights of Achi Baba. Between him and his objective were the spurs of that mountain stretching southward to the Gulf of Saros, and southward to the shores of the Straits. The enemy occupied the slopes of these spurs—slopes which were covered by dense scrub, which concealed from our fire innumerable parties of snipers, who had been well placed, and in some places had been provisioned for a month. The uneven character of the ground rendered our task the more difficult, deep gullies allowing not only of easy defence, but of the free movement of troops, and these had to be carried by the bayonet.

With the sniper our method was more elementary. He had to be hunted out, man by man, and for this purpose the Indian troops were employed. Wriggling forward foot by foot, the stalker, having located his prey, grew nearer and nearer to the doomed man; then, before he could realise his danger, a lithe, brown shape would leap from the underbrush, knife in hand, and the struggle would be sharp and short.

The British were on the left and the French on the right of the line in the attack, which was delivered through the village of Krithia toward Achi Baba. The front was a confined one, limited to the littoral on either side of the Peninsula. Warships posted in the Gulf and in the Straits opened the engagement by directing a heavy and searching fire along the entrenched slopes of the spur. It was a remarkable sight; the whole of the hill seemed to be in flame as 12- and 6-inch shell burst continuously above the Turks' position. The eighty-seventh British brigade held the deep gully to the left and the trenches on the hills beyond, whilst on their right was the eighty-eighth brigade. The Naval Division were across the Krithia road and to the right of that road. The line was continued by the French, Senegalese in the centre, a French infantry division on their right, and the reserves were the Indian Brigade, the Australians and New Zealanders, the Territorial Division that had just arrived on the Peninsula, the Zouaves, and the Foreign Legion. Krithia itself stands on a ridge, and the immediate objective of the British was to capture this town, which would very largely and very materially assist in the domination of Achi Baba. The fight was opened by the French 75's, which maintained a fierce bombardment of the country on their immediate front and of the trenches which the Turks were occupying to the right of the Krithia road. It was such a thorough bombardment as was generally seen at the beginning of the war, searching every yard of the ground, whilst the battleships in the Dardanelles as effectively raked the upper slopes of Achi Baba.

For thirty minutes this bombardment was kept up, and then the Senegalese swept out of their trenches and raced forward in open order up the right slope of the mountain. The extraordinary accuracy of the French gunfire was never better exemplified than in that charge, for as the Senegalese ran so did the "seventy- fives" drop a curtain of shrapnel fifty yards ahead of them, and between them and their enemy. They gained the crest of the rise, but here they had need to dig themselves in, for on the far slope they were held up by the Turkish entrenchments. The Royal Naval Division, which had spent the winter of 1914 in training at the Crystal Palace, came into action next, advancing across the broken ground under a heavy fire. They were not held up until they struck the entanglements of the Turks' trenches. It was, however, a serious hold-up, and immediately the ships were signalled as to its cause. Instantly the whole fleet in the vicinity turned its guns upon the patch of scrub in which the Turk was concealed. Nothing, however, silenced the Turkish fire, and the advance was stopped for that day. The following morning, after a heavy bombardment of the Turkish position, the eighty-seventh and eighty-eighth brigades pressed forward, but came under a particularly violent fusillade from the concealed German trenches. Notwithstanding this, our infantry moved forward, carried a line of the enemy's trenches and occupied them. It was not till three in the afternoon that the French again moved. The intervening time had been marked by heavy exchanges of artillery fire, the Turks being particularly energetic in their attack upon our reserves. The Turks were now apparently bringing every gun they possessed into action against our Ally, and the French batteries replied in kind.

Under cover of the French fire their infantry moved forward only to be driven back, and for a time the situation was critical. The Foreign Legion, which had been in reserve, was now brought forward to the front line. The bombardment by combined ships and the full strength of the Allies' artillery was resumed, and at six o'clock in the evening the British went forward, gained yet another stretch of ground, and in the gathering darkness dug themselves in. The next morning was to see a renewal of the advance of an even more violent character than either of the previous days. It opened, as usual, by a tremendous bombardment of the right spur of Achi Baba by the heavy guns. For thirty minutes this inferno of flame and splintering shell was poured upon the Turks' position before our infantry again advanced, and again were met by withering fire from rifle, field gun and machine gun. The eighty-seventh and eighty-eighth did not waver, but went straight at the trench before them, and carried the whole line with splendid dash.

Soon afterwards the New Zealanders, who had been in reserve, moved up to take their place in the final assault, whilst the Australian brigade, which had relieved the Naval Brigade for the same purpose, came into the front line in the centre. For four hours in the afternoon of May 8th it seemed as if a temporary truce had been proclaimed, for there was no evidence of life on either side, save the monotonous crack of the sniper's rifle; but at five o'clock such a bombardment was opened upon the Turkish line as had not been known in the history of war.

Every ship that could be spared for the purpose closed in to the shore, and heavy armament, no less than secondary armament, was requisitioned for this, the most terrible artillery assault. Both arms of Achi Baba were subjected to this rain of fire. 15-inch and 12-inch shells charged with lyddite splattered the face of the hill scarlet and yellow.

"They were spraying Achi Baba as you spray a flower-bed with water. Not a single inch seemed to escape this systematic search. Every gunner in every ship had been allotted a certain section of ground to cover, and it was impossible to see the hill for bursting flame."

To the second the bombardment ceased, and again the infantry, which had been lying concealed in the shrub or in the cover of their trenches, moved forward to one grand assault.

"No sooner had our men emerged from cover than a perfect storm of rifle and machine gun fire was opened upon them from the trenches and shrub over which the shells had burst and were still bursting," wrote the official correspondent. "The rifle fire rose fast into one continuous roar, only broken by the more rapid note of the machine guns. But our men never hesitated for a moment. The New Zealanders hurled themselves forward in a solid phalanx, passing through the eighty-eighth brigade, and many of the gallant men of those regiments, refusing to yield any right of way to them, joined their ranks and rushed forward in a thin, mad charge.

"The line entered one Turkish trench with a rush, bayoneted all there, and then passed on into broken ground, shooting and stabbing, men falling amidst a terrible fusillade, but not a soul turning back. No sooner had one line charged than another pressed on after it, and then a third.

"On the right of the New Zealanders the Australians advanced at the same moment, but over much more open ground, which provided little or no cover. They were met by a tornado of bullets, and were enfiladed by machine guns from the right, and the artillery in vain endeavoured to keep down this fire.

"The manner in which these Dominion troops went forward will never be forgotten by those who witnessed it. The lines of infantry were enveloped in dust from the patter of countless bullets in the sandy soil and from the hail of shrapnel poured on them, for now the enemy's artillery concentrated furiously on the whole line.

"The lines advanced steadily as if on parade, sometimes doubling, sometimes walking, and you saw them melt away under this dreadful fusillade, only to be renewed again as the reserves and supports moved forward to replace those who had fallen.

"In spite of all obstacles a considerable advance towards Krithia was made, but at length a point was reached from which it was impossible to proceed further. Not a man attempted to return to the trenches. They simply lay down where they were and attempted to reply to their concealed enemy, not one of whom disclosed his position. These Australians and New Zealanders were determined not to budge, and proceeded to entrench themselves where they were. But it became obvious at the end of an hour that the attack had spent its force, and that the hope of taking Krithia by direct assault must be abandoned."

The ground won amounted to no more than a few hundred yards, but what had been taken was held.

The honours of those three days cannot well be divided.

French, British, Senegalese, Australian, New Zealand and Indian troops fought side by side with the Naval men and that most extraordinary corps, the Foreign Legion.

The Australian showed himself reckless of danger, and, in the face of a terribly punishing fire, was as steady as the oldest soldier. Here, too, the Naval Brigade, which had been under the command of the French General d'Amade, earned the praise of that gallant commander—praise which was indeed well earned.

To many of the Territorials who took part in that fight it was a terrible baptism of fire, yet they behaved with the courage and sang froid of men who were inured to war. Our losses were heavy, but here again we have evidence that the Turk, for all the resistance he put up—and it was a magnificent resistance—suffered enormously. From an authoritative source it was learnt that 40,000 Turks were put out of action in those three days of fighting. Certainly the heavy shelling to which they were subjected must have caused enormous losses, and the holding up of our advance was probably due to the dauntless resistance of Turkish infantry who, because of the concealed position of their trenches, had escaped the devastating shelling which their less fortunate fellows had received. The force which von Goltz commanded was 200,000 men, and his losses were such as to necessitate the bringing forward from Constantinople of another 50,000. With 40,000 men on each mile of his front, it follows that the difficulty of forcing a way through was an enormous one, if indeed one which was not altogether impossible.

In the final advance a platoon (fifty men) of Australians found themselves cut off from the rest of their regiment and subjected to a fire from three sides. A retirement to their line could only be carried out at the risk of very heavy losses, and the Australians decided to charge forward at the trench on their front, from whence most of the firing came, and this they did, occupying and holding the enemy's trench till under cover of darkness they were able to withdraw to a less parlous position.

The desperate fighting of these three days had emphasised still further the gigantic difficulties of the task before the Allies. "Everywhere," as the official correspondent pointed out, "we had gained some ground, but the main object of the attack had not yet been achieved. Achi Baba still looked defiantly on the plain beneath, and it was obvious that such strong positions as the Turks held could only be won by extreme patience."

And he might have added by the unwearying support of the Navy, which, despite the arrival on the scene of German submarines, were as constantly in attendance as ever.

In an appendix is produced General Sir Ian Hamilton's account of the landing. No more memorable or better deserved tribute has been paid to the Senior Service that that which is contained in the sentence: "The Royal Navy has been father and mother to the Army."

APPENDIX. — SIR IAN HAMILTON'S DESPATCH

From the General Commanding the Mediterranean Expeditionary Force.
To the Secretary of State for War, War Office, London, S.W.

General Headquarters, Mediterranean Expeditionary Force,

May 20th, 1915.

My Lord

I have the honour to submit my report on the operations in the Gallipoli Peninsula up to and including May 5th.

In accordance with your Lordship's instructions I left London on March 13th with my General Staff by special train to Marseilles, and thence in H.M.S. Phaeton to the scene of the naval operations in the Eastern Mediterranean, reaching Tenedos on March 17th shortly after noon.

Immediately on arrival I conferred with Vice-Admiral de Robeck, commanding the Eastern Mediterranean Fleet; General d'Amade, commanding the French Corps Expéditionnaire; and Contre Amiral Guepratte, in command of the French Squadron. At this conference past difficulties were explained to me, and the intention to make a fresh attack on the morrow was announced. The amphibious battle between warships and land fortresses took place next day, March 18th. I witnessed these stupendous events, and thereupon cabled your Lordship my reluctant deduction that the co-operation of the whole of the force under my command would be required to enable the Fleet effectively to force the Dardanelles.

By that time I had already carried out a preliminary reconnaissance of the north-western shore of the Gallipoli Peninsula, from its isthmus, where it is spanned by the Bulair fortified lines, to Cape Helles, at its extremest point. From Bulair this singular feature runs in a south-westerly direction for fifty- two miles, attaining near its centre a breadth of twelve miles. The northern coast of the northern half of the promontory slopes downwards steeply to the Gulf of Xeros, in a chain of hills, which extend as far as Cape Sulva. The precipitous fall of these hills precludes landing, except at a few narrow gullies, far too restricted for any serious military movements. The southern half of the peninsula is shaped like a badly-worn boot. The ankle lies between Gaba Tepe and Kalkmaz Dagh; beneath the heel lie the cluster of forts at Kilid Bahr; whilst the toe is that promontory five miles in width, stretching from Tekke Bumu to Sedd-el-Bahr.

The three dominating features in this southern section seemed to me to be:—

(1) Saribair Mountain, running up in a succession of almost perpendicular escarpments to 970 feet. The whole mountain seemed to be a network of ravines and covered with thick jungle.

(2) Kilid Bahr plateau, which rises, a natural fortification artificially fortified, to a height of 700 feet to cover the forts of the Narrows from an attack from the Aegean.

(3) Achi Babi, a hill 600 feet in height, dominating at long field gun range what I have described as being the toe of the peninsula.

A peculiarity to be noted as regards this last southern sector is that from Achi Babi to Cape Helles the ground is hollowed out like a spoon, presenting only its outer edges to direct fire from the sea. The inside of the spoon appears to be open and undulating, but actually it is full of spurs, nullahs, and confused underfeatures.

Generally speaking the coast is precipitous, and good landing-places are few. Just south of Tekke Bumu is a small sandy bay (referred to subsequently as "W"), and half a mile north of it is another small break in the cliffs (referred to subsequently as "X"). Two miles farther up the coast the mouth of a stream indents these same cliffs (referred to subsequently as "Y 2"), and yet another mile and a half up a scrub-covered gully looked as if active infantry might be able to scramble up it on to heights not altogether dissimilar to those of Abraham, by Quebec (Y.). Inside Sedd-el-Bahr is a sandy beach (V), about 300 yards across, facing a semi-circle of steeply-rising ground, as the flat bottom of a half-saucer faces the rim, a rim flanked on one side by an old castle, on the other by a modern fort. By Eski Hissarlik, on the east of Morto Bay (S), was another small beach, which was, however, dominated by the big guns from Asia. Turning northwards again, there are two good landing places on either side of Gaba Tepe. Farther to the north of that promontory the beach was supposed to be dangerous and difficult. In most of these landing-places the trenches and lines of wire entanglements were plainly visible from on board ship. What seemed to be gun emplacements and infantry redoubts could also be made out through a telescope, but of the full extent of these defences and of the forces available to man them there was no possibility of judging except by practical test.

Altogether the result of this and subsequent reconnaissances was to convince me that nothing but a thorough and systematic scheme for flinging the whole of the troops under my command very rapidly ashore could be expected to meet with success; whereas, on the other hand, a tentative or piecemeal programme was bound to lead to disaster. The landing of an army upon the theatre of operations I have described—a theatre strongly garrisoned throughout, and prepared for any such attempt—involved difficulties for which no precedent was forthcoming in military history except possibly in the sinister legends of Xerxes. The beaches were either so well defended by works and guns or else so restricted by nature that it did not seem possible, even by two or three simultaneous landings, to pass the troops ashore quickly enough to enable them to maintain themselves against the rapid concentration and counterattack which the enemy was bound in such case to attempt. It became necessary, therefore, not only to land simultaneously at as many points as possible, but to threaten to land at other points as well. The first of these necessities involved another unavoidable if awkward contingency, the separation by considerable intervals of the force.

The weather was also bound to play a vital part in my landing. Had it been British weather there would have been no alternative but instantly to give up the adventure. To land two or three thousand men, and then to have to break off and leave them exposed for a week to the attacks of 34,000 regular troops, with a hundred guns at their back, was not an eventuality to be lightly envisaged. Whatever happened, the weather must always remain an incalculable factor, but at least by delay till the end of April we had a fair chance of several days of consecutive calm.

Before doing anything else I had to redistribute the troops on the transports to suit the order of their disembarkation. The bulk of the forces at my disposal had, perforce, been embarked without its having been possible to pay due attention to the operation upon which I now proposed that they should be launched.

Owing to lack of facilities at Mudros redistribution in that harbour was out of the question. With your Lordship's approval, therefore, I ordered all the transports, except those of the Australian Infantry Brigade and the details encamped at Lemnos Island, to the Egyptian ports. On March 24th I myself, together with the General Staff, proceeded to Alexandria, where I remained until April 7th, working out the allocation of troops to transports in minutest details as a prelude to the forthcoming disembarkation. General d'Amade did likewise.

On April 1st the remainder of the General Headquarters, which had not been mobilised when I left England, arrived at Alexandria.

Apart from the re-arrangements of the troops, my visit to Egypt was not without profit, since it afforded me opportunities of conferring with the G.O.C. Egypt and of making myself acquainted with the troops, drawn from all parts of the French Republic and of the British Empire, which it was to be my privilege to command.

By April 7th my preparations were sufficiently advanced to enable me to return with my General Staff to Lemnos, so as to put the finishing touches to my plan in close co-ordination with the Vice-Admiral Commanding the Eastern Mediterranean Fleet.
The covering force of the 29th Division left Mudros Harbour on the evening of April 23rd for the five beaches, S, V, W, X, and Y. Of these, V, W, and X were to be main landings, the landings at S and Y being made mainly to protect the flanks, to disseminate the forces of the enemy, and to interrupt the arrival of his reinforcements. The landings at S and Y were to take place at dawn, whilst it was planned that the first troops for V, W, and X beaches should reach the shore simultaneously at 5.30 a.m. after half an hour's bombardment from the Fleet.

The transports conveying the covering force arrived off Tenedos on the morning of the 24th, and during the afternoon the troops were transferred to the warships and fleet-sweepers in which they were to approach the shore. About midnight these ships, each towing a number of cutters and other small boats, silently slipped their cables and, escorted by the 3rd Squadron of the Fleet, steamed slowly towards their final rendezvous at Cape Helles. The rendezvous was reached just before dawn on the 25th. The morning was absolutely still; there was no sign of life on the shore; a thin veil of mist hung motionless over the promontory; the surface of the sea was as smooth as glass.

The four battleships and four cruisers which formed the 3rd Squadron at once took up the positions that had been allotted to them, and at 5 a.m., it being then light enough to fire, a violent bombardment of the enemy's defences was begun. Meanwhile the troops were being rapidly transferred to the small boats in which they were to be towed ashore. Not a move on the part of the enemy; except for shells thrown from the Asiatic side of the Straits the guns of the Fleet remained unanswered.

The detachment detailed for S beach (Eski Hissarlik Point) consisted of the 2nd South Wales Borderers (less one company) under Lieut Colonel Casson. Their landing was delayed by the current, but by 7.30 a.m. it had been successfully effected at the cost of some 50 casualties, and Lieut.-Colonel Casson was able to establish his small force on the high ground near De Totts Battery. Here he maintained himself until the general advance on the 27th brought him into touch with the main body.

The landing on Y beach was entrusted to the King's Own Scottish Borderers and the Plymouth (Marine) Battalion, Royal Naval Division, specially attached to the 29th Division for this task, the whole under the command of Lieut.-Colonel Koe. The beach at this point consisted merely of a narrow strip of sand at the foot of a crumbling scrub-covered cliff some 200 feet high immediately to the west of Krithia.

A number of small gullies running down the face of the cliff facilitated the climb to the summit, and so impracticable had these precipices appeared to the Turks that no steps had been taken to defend them. Very different would it have been had we, as was at one time intended, taken Y 2 for this landing. There a large force of infantry, entrenched up to their necks, and supported by machine and Hotchkiss guns, were awaiting an attempt which could hardly have made good its footing. But at Y both battalions were able in the first instance to establish themselves on the heights, reserves of food, water, and ammunition were hauled up to the top of the cliff, and, in accordance with the plan of operations, an endeavour was immediately made to gain touch with the troops landing at X beach. Unfortunately, the enemy's strong detachment from Y 2 interposed, our troops landing at X were fully occupied in attacking the Turks immediately to their front, and the attempt to join hands was not persevered with.

Later in the day a large force of Turks were seen to be advancing upon the cliffs above Y beach, from the direction of Krithia, and Colonel Koe was obliged to entrench. From this time onward his small force was subjected to strong and repeated attacks, supported by field artillery, and owing to the configuration of the ground, which here drops inland from the edge of the cliff, the guns of the supporting ships could render him little assistance. Throughout the afternoon and all through the night the Turks made assault after assault upon the British line.
They threw bombs into the trenches, and, favoured by darkness, actually led a pony with a machine gun on its back over the defences and were proceeding to come into action in the middle of our position when they were bayoneted.

The British repeatedly counter-charged with the bayonet, and always drove off the enemy for the moment, but the Turks were in a vast superiority and fresh troops took the place of those who temporarily fell back. Colonel Koe (since died of wounds) had become a casualty early in the day, and the number of officers and men killed and wounded during the incessant fighting was very heavy. By 7 a.m. on the 26th only about half of the King's Own Scottish Borderers remained to man the entrenchment made for four times their number. These brave fellows were absolutely worn out with continuous fighting; it was doubtful if reinforcements could reach them in time, and orders were issued for them to be re-embarked. Thanks to H.M.S. Goliath, Dublin, Amethyst, and Sapphire, thanks also to the devotion of a small rearguard of the King's Own Scottish Borderers, which kept off the enemy from lining the cliff, the re- embarkation of the whole of the troops, together with the wounded, stores, and ammunition, was safely accomplished, and both battalions were brought round the southern end of the peninsula. Deplorable as the heavy losses had been, and unfortunate as was the tactical failure to make good so much ground at the outset, yet, taking the operation as it stood, there can be no doubt it has contributed greatly to the success of the main attack, seeing that the plucky stand made at Y beach had detained heavy columns of the enemy from arriving at the southern end of the peninsula during what it will be seen was a very touch and go struggle.

The landing-place known as X beach consists of a strip of sand some 200 yards long by eight yards wide at the foot of a low cliff. The troops to be landed here were the 1st Royal Fusiliers, who were to be towed ashore from H.M.S. Implacable in two parties, half a battalion at a time, together with a beach working party found by the Anson Battalion, Royal Naval Division. About 6 a.m. H.M.S. Implacable, with a boldness much admired by the Army, stood quite close in to the beach, firing very rapidly with every gun she could bring to bear. Thus seconded, the Royal Fusiliers made good their landing with but little loss. The battalion then advanced to attack the Turkish trenches on the Hill 114, situated between V and W beaches, but were heavily counter-attacked and forced to give ground.

Two more battalions of the 87th Brigade soon followed them, and by evening the troops had established themselves in an entrenched position extending from half a mile round the landing-place and as far south as Hill 114. Here they were in touch with the Lancashire Fusiliers, who had landed on W beach. Brigadier- General Marshall, commanding the 87th Brigade, had been wounded during the day's fighting, but continued in command of the brigade.

The landing on V beach was planned to take place on the following lines:—

As soon as the enemy's defences had been heavily bombarded by the Fleet, three companies of the Dublin Fusiliers, were to be towed ashore. They were to be closely followed by the collier River Clyde (Commander Unwin, R.N.), carrying between decks the balance of the Dublin Fusiliers, the Munster Fusiliers, half a battalion of the Hampshire Regiment, the West Riding Field Company, and other details.

The River Clyde had been specially prepared for the rapid disembarkation of her complement, and large openings for the exit of the troops had been cut in her sides, giving on to a wide gang-plank by which the men could pass rapidly into lighters which she had in tow. As soon as the first tows had reached land the River Clyde was to be run straight ashore. Her lighters were to be placed in position to form a gangway between the ship and the beach, and by this means it was hoped that 2,000 men could be thrown ashore with the utmost rapidity. Further, to assist in covering the landing, a battery of machine guns, protected by sandbags, had been mounted in her bows.

The remainder of the covering force detailed for this beach was then to follow in tows from the attendant battleships.

V beach is situated immediately to the west of Sedd-el-Bahr. Between the bluff on which stands Sedd-el-Bahr village and that which is crowned by No. 1 fort the ground forms a very regular amphitheatre of three or four hundred yards' radius. The slopes down to the beach are slightly concave, so that the whole area contained within the limits of this natural amphitheatre, whose grassy terraces rise gently to a height of a hundred feet above the shore, can be swept by the fire of a defender. The beach itself is a sandy strip some ten yards wide and 350 yards long, backed along almost the whole of its extent by a low sandy escarpment about four feet high, where the ground falls nearly sheer down to the beach. The slight shelter afforded by this escarpment played no small part in the operations of the succeeding thirty-two hours.

At the south-eastern extremity of the beach, between the shore and the village, stands the old fort of Sedd-el-Bahr, a battered ruin with wide breaches in its walls and mounds of fallen masonry within and around it. On the ridge to the north, overlooking the amphitheatre, stands a ruined barrack. Both of these buildings, as well as No. 1 fort, had been long bombarded by the Fleet, and the guns of the forts had been put out of action; but their crumbled walls and the ruined outskirts of the village afforded cover for riflemen, while from the terraced slopes already described the defenders were able to command the open beach, as a stage is overlooked from the balconies of a theatre. On the very margin of the beach a strong barbed-wire entanglement, made of heavier metal and longer barbs than I have ever seen elsewhere, ran right across from the old fort of Sedd-el-Bahr to the foot of the north- western headland. Two-thirds of the way up the ridge a second and even stronger entanglement crossed the amphitheatre, passing in front of the old barrack and ending in the outskirts of the village. A third transverse entanglement, joining these two, ran up the hill near the eastern end of the beach, and almost at right angles to it. Above the upper entanglement the ground was scored with the enemy's trenches, in one of which four pom-poms were emplaced; in others were dummy pom-poms to draw fire, while the débris of the shattered buildings on either flank afforded cover and concealment for a number of machine guns, which brought a cross-fire to bear on the ground already swept by rifle-fire from the ridge.

Needless to say, the difficulties in the way of previous reconnaissance had rendered it impossible to obtain detailed information with regard either to the locality or to the enemy's preparations. As often happens in war, the actual course of events did not quite correspond with the intentions of the Commander The River Clyde came into position off Sedd-el-Bahr in advance of the tows, and, just as the latter reached the shore, Commander Unwin beached his ship also. Whilst the boats and the collier were approaching the landing place the Turks made no sign. Up to the very last moment it appeared as if the landing was to be unopposed. But the moment the first boat touched bottom the storm broke. A tornado of fire swept over the beach, the incoming boats, and the collier. The Dublin Fusiliers, and the naval boats' crews suffered exceedingly heavy losses while still in the boats. Those who succeeded in landing and in crossing the strip of sand managed to gain some cover when they reached the low escarpment on the further side. None of the boats, however, were able to get off again, and they and their crews were destroyed upon the beach.

Now came the moment for the River Clyde to pour forth her living freight; but grievous delay was caused here by the difficulty of placing the lighters in position between the ship and the shore. A strong current hindered the work, and the enemy's fire was so intense that almost every man engaged upon it was immediately shot. Owing, however, to the splendid gallantry of the naval working party, the lighters were eventually placed in position, and then the disembarkation began.

A company of the Munster Fusiliers led the way; but, short as was the distance, few of the men ever reached the farther side of the beach through the hail of bullets which poured down upon them from both flanks and the front. As the second company followed, the extemporised pier of lighters gave way in the current. The end nearest to the shore drifted into deep water, and many men who had escaped being shot were drowned by the weight of their equipment in trying to swim from the lighter to the beach. Undaunted workers were still forthcoming, the lighters were again brought into position, and the third company of the Munster Fusiliers rushed ashore, suffering heaviest loss this time from shrapnel as well as from rifle, pom-pom, and machine-gun fire.

For a space the attempt to land was discontinued. When it was resumed the lighters again drifted into deep water, with Brigadier-General Napier, Captain Costeker, his Brigade Major, and a number of men of the Hampshire Regiment on board. There was nothing for them all but to lie down on the lighters, and it was here that General Napier and Captain Costeker were killed. At this time, between 10 and ii a.m., about 1,000 men had left the collier, and of these nearly half had been killed or wounded before they could reach the little cover afforded by the steep, sandy bank at the top of the beach. Further attempts to disembark were now given up. Had the troops all been in open boats but few of them would have lived to tell the tale. But, most fortunately, the collier was so constructed as to afford fairly efficient protection to the men who were still on board, and so long as they made no attempt to land, they suffered comparatively little loss.

Throughout the remainder of the day there was practically no change in the position of affairs. The situation was probably saved by the machine-guns on the River Clyde, which did valuable service in keeping down the enemy's fire and in preventing any attempt on their part to launch a counter-attack. One half-company of the Dublin Fusiliers, which had been landed at a camber just east of Sedd-el-Bahr village, was unable to work its way across to V beach, and by mid-day had only twenty-five men left. It was proposed to divert to Y beach that part of the main body which had been intended to land on V beach; but this would have involved considerable delay owing to the distance, and the main body was diverted to W beach, where the Lancashire Fusiliers had already effected a landing.

Late in the afternoon part of the Worcestershire Regiment and the Lancashire Fusiliers worked across the high ground from W beach, and seemed likely to relieve the situation by taking the defenders of V beach in flank. The pressure on their own front, however, and the numerous barbed-wire entanglements which intervened, checked this advance, and at nightfall the Turkish garrison still held their ground. Just before dark some small parties of our men made their way along the shore to the outer walls of the Old Fort, and when night had fallen the remainder of the infantry from the collier were landed. A good force was now available for attack, but our troops were at such a cruel disadvantage as to position, and the fire of the enemy was still so accurate in the bright moonlight, that all attempts to clear the fort and the outskirts of the village during the night failed one after the other. The wounded who were able to do so without support returned to the collier under cover of darkness; but otherwise the situation at daybreak on the 26th was the same as it had been on the previous day, except that the troops first landed were becoming very exhausted.

Twenty-four hours after the disembarkation began there were ashore on V beach the survivors of the Dublin and Munster Fusiliers and of two companies of the Hampshire Regiment. The Brigadier and his Brigade Major had been killed; Lieutenant-Colonel Carrington Smith, commanding the Hampshire Regiment, had been killed and the adjutant had been wounded. The Adjutant of the Munster Fusiliers was wounded and the great majority of the senior officers were either wounded or killed. The remnant of the landing-party still crouched on the beach beneath the shelter of the sandy escarpment which had saved so many lives. With them were two officers of my General Staff—Lieutenant-Colonel Doughty- Wylie and Lieutenant-Colonel Williams. These two officers who had landed from the River Clyde, had been striving, with conspicuous contempt for danger, to keep all their comrades in good heart during this day and night of ceaseless imminent peril.

Now that it was daylight once more, Lieutenant-Colonels Doughty-Wylie and Williams set to work to organise an attack on the hill above the beach. Any soldier who has endeavoured to pull scattered units together after they have been dominated by many consecutive hours by close and continuous fire will be able to take the measure of their difficulties. Fortunately General Hunter- Weston had arranged with Rear-Admiral Wemyss about this same time for a heavy bombardment to be opened by the ships upon the Old Fort, Sedd-el-Bahr Village, the old Castle north of the village, and on the ground leading up from the beach. Under cover of this bombardment, and led by Lieutenant-Colonel Doughty Wylie, and Captain Walford, Brigade Major R.A., the troops gained a footing in the village by 10 a.m. They encountered a most stubborn opposition and suffered heavy losses from the fire of well concealed riflemen and machine-guns.

Undeterred by the resistance, and supported by the naval gunfire, they pushed forward, and soon after midday they penetrated to the northern edge of the village, whence they were in a position to attack the Old Castle and Hill 141. During this advance Captain Walford was killed. Lieutenant-Colonel Doughty- Wylie had most gallantly led the attack all the way up from the beach through the west side of the village, under a galling fire. And now, when, owing so largely to his own inspiring example and intrepid courage, the position had almost been gained, he was killed while leading the last assault. But the attack was pushed forward without wavering, and, fighting their way across the open with great dash, the troops gained the summit and occupied the Old Castle and Hill 141 before 2 p.m.

W beach consists of a strip of deep, powdery sand some 350 yards long and from 15 to 40 yards wide, situated immediately south of Tekke Burnu, where a small gully running down to the sea opens out a break in the cliffs. On either flank of the beach the ground rises precipitously, but, in the centre, a number of sand dunes afford a more gradual access to the ridge overlooking the sea. Much time and ingenuity had been employed by the Turks in turning this landing place into a death trap. Close to the water's edge a broad wire-entanglement extended the whole length of the shore and a supplementary barbed network lay concealed under the surface of the sea in the shallows. Land mines and sea mines had been laid. The high ground overlooking the beach was strongly fortified with trenches to which the gully afforded a natural covered approach. A number of machine guns also were cunningly tucked away into holes in the cliff so as to be immune from a naval bombardment whilst they were converging their fire on the wire entanglements. The crest of the hill overlooking the beach was in its turn commanded by high ground to the north-west and south-east, and especially by two strong infantry redoubts near point 138. Both these redoubts were protected by wire entanglements about 20 feet broad, and could be approached only by a bare glacis-like slope leading up from the high ground above W beach or from the Cape Helles lighthouse. In addition, another separate entanglement ran down from these two redoubts to the edge of the cliff near the lighthouse, making intercommunication between V and W beaches impossible until these redoubts had been captured.

So strong, in fact, were the defences of W beach that the Turks may well have considered them impregnable, and it is my firm conviction that no finer feat of arms has ever been achieved by the British soldier, or any other soldier, than the storming of these trenches from open boats on the morning of April 25.

The landing at W had been entrusted to the 1st Battalion Lancashire Fusiliers (Major Bishop), and it was to the complete lack of the senses of danger or of fear of this daring battalion that we owed our astonishing success. As in the case of the landing at X, the disembarkation had been delayed for half an hour, but at 6 a.m. the whole battalion approached the shore together, towed by eight picket boats in line abreast, each picket boat pulling four ship's cutters. As soon as shallow water was reached, the tows were cast off and the boats were at once rowed to the shore. Three companies headed for the beach and a company on the left of the line made for a small ledge of rock immediately under the cliff at Tekke Bumu. Brigadier-General Hare, commanding the 88th Brigade, accompanied this latter party, which escaped the cross fire brought to bear upon the beach, and was also in a better position than the rest of the battalion to turn the wire entanglements.

While the troops were approaching the shore no shot had been fired from the enemy's trenches, but as soon as the first boat touched the ground a hurricane of lead swept over the battalion. Gallantly led by their officers, the Fusiliers literally hurled themselves ashore, and, fired at from right, left, and centre, commenced hacking their way through the wire. A long line of men was at once mown down as by a scythe, but the remainder were not to be denied. Covered by the fire of the warships, which had now closed right in to the shore, and helped by the flanking fire of the company on the extreme left, they broke through the entanglements and collected under the cliffs on either side of the beach.

Here the companies were rapidly reformed, and set forth to storm the enemy's entrenchments wherever they could find them.

In making these attacks the bulk of the battalion moved up towards Hill 114, whilst a small party worked down towards the trenches on the Cape Helles side of the landing-place.

Several land mines were exploded by the Turks during the advance, but the determination of the troops was in no way affected. By 10 a.m. three lines of hostile trenches were in our hands, and our hold on the beach was assured.

About 9.30 a.m. more infantry had begun to disembark, and two hours later a- junction was effected on Hill 114 with the troops who had landed on X beach.

On the right, owing to the strength of the redoubt on Hill 138, little progress could be made. The small party of Lancashire Fusiliers which had advanced in this direction succeeded in reaching the edge of the wire entanglements, but were not strong enough to do more, and it was here that Major Frankland, Brigade Major of the 86th Infantry Brigade, who had gone forward to make a personal reconnaissance, was unfortunately killed. Brigadier- General Hare had been wounded earlier in the day, and Colonel Woolly-Dod, General Staff 29th Division, was now sent ashore to take command at W beach and organise a further advance.

At 2 p.m., after the ground near Hill 138 had been subjected to a heavy bombardment, the Worcester Regiment advanced to the assault. Several men of this battalion rushed forward with great spirit to cut passages through the entanglement; some were killed, others persevered, and by 4 p.m. the hill and redoubt were captured.

An attempt was now made to join hands with the troops on V beach, who could make no headway at all against the dominating defences of the enemy. To help them out the 86th Brigade pushed forward in an easterly direction along the cliff. There is a limit, however, to the storming of barbed-wire entanglements. More of these barred the way. Again the heroic wire-cutters came out. Through glasses they could be seen quietly snipping away under a hellish fire as if they were pruning a vineyard. Again some of them fell. The fire pouring out of No. 1 fort grew hotter and hotter, until the troops, now thoroughly exhausted by a sleepless night and by the long day's fighting under a hot sun, had to rest on their laurels for a while.

When night fell, the British position in front of W beach extended from just east of Cape Helles lighthouse, through Hill 138, to Hill 114. Practically every man had to be thrown into the trenches to hold this line, and the only available reserves on this part of our front were the 2nd London Field Company R.E. and a platoon of the Anson Battalion, which had been landed as a beach working party.

During the night several strong and determined counter-attacks were made, all successfully repulsed without loss of ground. Meanwhile the disembarkation of the remainder of the division was proceeding on W and X beaches.

The Australian and New Zealand Army Corps sailed out of Mudros Bay on the afternoon of April 24, escorted by the 2nd Squadron of the Fleet, under Rear- Admiral Thursby. The rendezvous was reached just after half-past one in the morning of the 25th, and there the 1,500 men who had been placed on board H.M. ships before leaving Mudros were transferred to their boats. This operation was carried out with remarkable expedition, and in absolute silence. Simultaneously the remaining 2,500 men of the covering force were transferred from their transports to six destroyers. At 2.30

a.m. H.M. ships, together with the tows and the destroyers, proceeded to within some four miles of the coast, H.M.S. Queen (flying Rear-Admiral Thursby's flag) directing on a point about a mile north of Kaba Tepe. At 3.30 a.m. orders to go ahead and land were given to the tows and at 4.10 a.m. the destroyers were ordered to follow.

All these arrangements worked without a hitch, and were carried out in complete orderliness and silence. No breath of wind ruffled the surface of the sea, and every condition was favourable save for the moon, which, sinking behind the ships, may have silhouetted them against its orb, betraying them thus to watchers on the shore.

A rugged and difficult part of the coast had been selected for the landing, so difficult and rugged that I considered the Turks were not at all likely to anticipate such a descent. Indeed, owing to the tows having failed to maintain their exact direction the actual point of disembarkation was rather more than a mile north of that which I had selected, and was more closely overhung by steeper cliffs. Although this accident increased the initial difficulty of driving the enemy off the heights inland, it has since proved itself to have been a blessing in disguise, inasmuch as the actual base of the force of occupation has been much better defiladed from shell fire.

The beach on which the landing was actually effected is a very narrow strip of sand, about 1,000 yards in length, bounded on the north and the south by two small promontories. At its southern extremity a deep ravine, with exceedingly steep, scrub-clad sides, runs inland in a north-easterly direction. Near the northern end of the beach a small but steep gully runs up into the hills at right angles to the shore. Between the ravine and the gully the whole of the beach is backed by the seaward face of the spur which forms the north-western side of the ravine. From the top of the spur the ground falls almost sheer except near the southern limit of the beach, where gentler slopes give access to the mouth of the ravine behind. Further inland lie in a tangled knot the under-features of Saribair, separated by deep ravines, which take a most confusing diversity of direction. Sharp spurs, covered with dense scrub, and falling away in many places in precipitous sandy cliffs, radiate from the principal mass of the mountain, from which they run north-west, west, south-west, and south to the coast.

The boats approached the land in the silence and the darkness, and they were close to the shore before the enemy stirred. Then about one battalion of Turks was seen running along the beach to intercept the lines of boats. At this so critical a moment the conduct of all ranks was most praiseworthy. Not a word was spoken—everyone remained perfectly orderly and quiet awaiting the enemy's fire, which sure enough opened, causing many casualties. The moment the boats touched land the Australians' turn had come. Like lightning they leapt ashore, and each man as he did so went straight as his bayonet at the enemy. So vigorous was the onslaught that the Turks made no attempt to withstand it and fled from ridge to ridge pursued by the Australian infantry.

This attack was carried out by the 3rd Australian Brigade, under Major (temporary Colonel) Sinclair Maclagan, D.S.O. The 1st and 2nd Brigades followed promptly, and were all disembarked by 2 p.m., by which time 12,000 men and two batteries of Indian Mountain Artillery had been landed. The disembarkation of further artillery was delayed owing to the fact that the enemy's heavy guns opened on the anchorage and forced the transports, which had been subjected to continuous shelling from his field guns, to stand farther out to sea.

The broken ground, the thick scrub, the necessity for sending any formed detachments post haste as they landed to the critical point of the moment, the headlong valour of scattered groups of the men who had pressed far further into the peninsula than had been intended—all these led to confusion and mixing up of units. Eventually the mixed crowd of fighting men, some advancing from the beach, others falling back before the oncoming Turkish supports, solidified into a semi-circular position with its right about a mile north of Gaba Tepe and its left on the high ground over Fisherman's Hut. During this period, parties of the 9th and 10th Battalions charged and put out of action three of the enemy's Krupp guns. During this period also the disembarkation of the Australian Division was being followed by that of the New Zealand and Australian Division (two brigades only).

From 11 a.m. to 3 p.m. the enemy, now reinforced to a strength of 20,000 men, attacked the whole line, making a specially strong effort against the 3rd Brigade and the left of the 2nd Brigade. This counter-attack was, however, handsomely repulsed with the help of the guns of H.M. ships. Between 5 and 6.30 p.m. a third most determined counter-attack was made against the 3rd Brigade, who held their ground with more than equivalent stubbornness. During the night again the Turks made constant attacks, and the 8th Battalion repelled a bayonet charge; but in spite of all the line held firm. The troops had had practically no rest on the night of the 24/25th; they had been fighting hard all day over most difficult country, and they had been subjected to heavy shrapnel fire in the open. Their casualties had been deplorably heavy. But, despite their losses and in spite of their fatigue, the morning of the 26th found them still in good heart and as full of fight as ever.

It is a consolation to know' that the Turks suffered still more seriously. Several times our machine guns got on to them in close formation, and the whole surrounding country is still strewn with their dead of this date.

The reorganisation of units and formations was impossible during the 26th and 27th owing to persistent attacks. An advance was impossible until a reorganisation could be effected, and it only remained to entrench the position gained and to perfect the arrangements for bringing up ammunition, water, and supplies to the ridges—in itself a most difficult undertaking. Four battalions of the Royal Naval Division were sent up to reinforce the Army Corps on the 28th and 29th April. On the night of May 2nd a bold effort was made to seize a commanding knoll in front of the centre of the line. The enemy's enfilading machine guns were too scientifically posted, and 800 men were lost without advantage beyond the infliction of a corresponding loss to the enemy. On May 4th an attempt to seize Kaba Tepe was also unsuccessful, the barbed wire here being something beyond belief. But a number of minor operations have been carried out, such as the taking of a Turkish observing station; the strengthening of entrenchments; the reorganisation of units, and the perfecting of communication with the landing- place. Also a constant strain has been placed upon some of the best troops of the enemy, who, to the number of 24,000, are constantly kept fighting and being killed and wounded freely, as the Turkish sniper is no match for the Kangaroo shooter, even at his own game.

The assistance of the Royal Navy, here as elsewhere, has been invaluable. The whole of the arrangements have been in Admiral Thursby's hands, and I trust I may be permitted to say what a trusty and powerful friend he has proved himself to be to the Australian and New Zealand Army Corps.

Concurrently with the British landings a regiment of the French Corps was successfully disembarked at Kum Kale under the guns of the French Fleet, and remained ashore till the morning of the 26th, when they were re-embarked; 500 prisoners were captured by the French on this day.

This operation drew the fire of the Asiatic guns from Morto Bay and V beach on to Kum Kale, and contributed largely to the success of the British landings.

On the evening of the 26th the main disembarkation of the French Corps was begun, V beach being allotted to our Allies for this purpose, and it was arranged that the French should hold the portion of the front between the telegraph wire and the sea.

The following day I ordered a general advance to a line stretching from Hill 236 near Eski Hissarlik Point to the mouth of the stream two miles north of Tekke Bumu. This advance, which was commenced at midday, was completed without opposition, and the troops at once consolidated their new line. The forward movement relieved the growing congestion on the beaches, and by giving us possession of several new wells afforded a temporary solution to the water problem, which had hitherto been causing me much anxiety.

By the evening of the 27th the Allied Forces had established themselves on a line some three miles long, which stretched from the mouth of the nullah, 3,200 yards north-east of Tekke Burnu, to Eski Hissarlik Point, the three brigades of the 29th Division less two battalions on the left and in the centre, with four French battalions on the right, and beyond them again the South Wales Borderers on the extreme right.

Owing to casualties this line was somewhat thinly held. Still, it was so vital to make what headway we could before the enemy recovered himself and received fresh reinforcements that it was decided to push on as quickly as possible. Orders were therefore issued for a general advance to commence at 8 a.m. next day.

The 29th Division were to march on Krithia, with their left brigade leading, the French were directed to extend their left in conformity with the British movements, and to retain their right on the coastline south of the Kereves Dere.

The advance commenced at 8 a.m. on the 28th, and was carried out with commendable vigour, despite the fact that from the moment of landing the troops had been unable to obtain any proper rest.

The 87th Brigade, with which had been incorporated the Drake Battalion, Royal Naval Division, in the place of the King's Own Scottish Borderers and South Wales Borderers, pushed on rapidly, and by 10 a.m. had advanced some two miles. Here the further progress of the Border Regiment was barred by a strong work on the left flank. They halted to concentrate and make dispositions to attack it, and at that moment had to withstand a determined counterattack by the Turks. Aided by heavy gun fire from H.M.S. Queen Elizabeth, they succeeded in beating off the attack, but they made no further progress that day, and when night fell, entrenched themselves on the ground they had gained in the morning.

The Inniskilling Fusiliers, who advanced with their right on the Krithia ravine, reached a point about three-quarters of a mile south-west of Krithia. This was, however, the farthest limit attained, and later on in the day they fell back into line with other corps.

The 88th Brigade on the right of the 87th progressed steadily until about 11.30 a.m., when the stubbornness of the opposition, coupled with a dearth of ammunition, brought their advance to a standstill. The 86th Brigade, under Lieutenant Colonel Casson, which had been held in reserve, were thereupon ordered to push forward through the 88th Brigade in the direction of Krithia.

The movement commenced at about 1 p.m., but though small reconnoitring parties got to within a few hundred yards of Krithia, the main body of the Brigade did not get beyond the line held by the 88th Brigade. Meanwhile, the French had also pushed on in the face of strong opposition along the spurs on the western bank of the Kereves Dere, and had got to within a mile of Krithia with their right thrown back and their left in touch with the 88th Brigade. Here they were unable to make further progress; gradually the strength of the resistance made itself felt, and our Allies were forced during the afternoon to give ground.

By 2 p.m. the whole of the troops with the exception of the Drake Battalion had been absorbed into the firing line. The men were exhausted, and the few guns landed at the time were unable to afford them adequate artillery support. The small amount of transport available did not suffice to maintain the supply of munitions, and cartridges were running short despite all efforts to push them up from the landing places.

Hopes of getting a footing on Achi Babi had now perforce to be abandoned—at least for this occasion. The best that could be expected was that we should be able to maintain what we had won, and when at 3 p.m. the Turks made a determined counter-attack with the bayonet against the centre and right of our line, even this seemed exceedingly doubtful. Actually a partial retirement did take place. The French were also forced back, and at 6 p.m. orders were issued for our troops to entrench themselves as best they could in the positions they then held, with their right flank thrown back so as to maintain connection with our Allies. In this retirement the right flank of the 88th Brigade was temporarily uncovered, and the Worcester Regiment suffered severely.

Had it been possible to push in reinforcements in men, artillery, and munitions during the day, Krithia should have fallen, and much subsequent fighting for its capture would have been avoided. Two days later this would have been feasible, but I had to reckon with the certainty that the enemy would, in that same time, have received proportionately greater support. I was faced by the usual choice of evils, and although the result was not what I had hoped, I have no reason to believe that hesitation and delay would better have answered my purpose.

For, after all, we had pushed forward quite appreciably on the whole. The line eventually held by our troops on the night of the 28th ran from a point on the coast three miles north-west of Tekke Bumu to a point one mile north of Eski Hissarlik, whence it was continued by the French south-east to the coast.
Much inevitable mixing of units of the 86th and 88th Brigades had occurred during the day's fighting, and there was a dangerous re-entrant in the line at the junction of the 87th and 88th Brigades near the Krithia nullah. The French lost heavily, especially in officers, and required time to reorganise. The 29th April was consequently spent in straightening the line, and in consolidating and strengthening the positions gained. There was a certain amount of artillery and musketry fire, but nothing serious.

Similarly, on the 30th, no advance was made, nor was any attack delivered by the enemy. The landing of the bulk of the artillery was completed, and a readjustment of the line took place, the portion held by the French being somewhat increased.

Two more battalions of the Royal Naval Division had been disembarked, and these, together with three battalions of the 88th Brigade withdrawn from the line, were formed into a reserve.
This reserve was increased on May 1st by the addition of the 29th Indian Infantry Brigade, which released the three battalions of the 88th Brigade to return to the trenches. The Corps Expéditionnaire d'Orient had disembarked the whole of their infantry and all but two of their batteries by the same evening.

At 10 p.m. the Turks opened a hot shell fire upon our position, and half an hour later, just before the rise of the moon, they delivered a series of desperate attacks. Their formation was in three solid lines, the men in the front rank being deprived of ammunition to make them rely only upon the bayonet. The officers were served out with coloured Bengal lights to fire from their pistols, red indicating to the Turkish guns that they were to lengthen their range; green that our main position had been carried. The Turkish attack was to crawl on hands and knees until the time came for the final rush to be made. An eloquent hortative was signed von Zowenstern and addressed to the Turkish rank and file, who were called upon, by one mighty effort, to fling us all back into the sea. "Attack the enemy with the bayonet and utterly destroy him!

"We shall not retire one step; for, if we do, our religion, our country, and our nation will perish!

"Soldiers! The world is looking at you! Your only hope of salvation is to bring this battle to a successful issue or gloriously to give up your life in the attempt!"

The first momentum of this ponderous onslaught fell upon the right of the 86th Brigade, an unlucky spot, seeing all the officers thereabouts had already been killed or wounded. So when the Turks came right on without firing and charged into the trenches with the bayonet they made an ugly gap in the line. This gap was instantly filled by the 5th Royal Scots (Territorials), who faced to their flank and executed a brilliant bayonet charge against the enemy, and by the Essex Regiment detached for the purpose by the Officer Commanding 88th Brigade. The rest of the British line held its own with comparative ease, and it was not found necessary to employ any portion of the reserve. The storm next broke in fullest violence against the French left, which was held by the Senegalese. Behind them were two British Field Artillery Brigades and a Howitzer Battery. After several charges and counter-charges the Senegalese began to give ground, and a company of the Worcester Regiment and some gunners were sent forward to hold the gap. Later, a second company of the Worcester Regiment was also sent up, and the position was then maintained for the remainder of the night, although about 2 a.m. it was found necessary to dispatch one battalion Royal Naval Division to strengthen the extreme right of the French.

About 5 a.m. a counter-offensive was ordered, and the whole line began to advance. By 7.30 a.m. the British left had gained some 500 yards, and the centre had pushed the enemy back and inflicted heavy losses. The right also had gained some ground in conjunction with the French left, but the remainder of the French line was unable to progress. As the British centre and left were now subjected to heavy cross fire from concealed machine guns, it was found impossible to maintain the ground gained, and therefore, about 11 a.m., the whole line withdrew to its former trenches.
The net result of the operations was the repulse of the Turks and the infliction upon them of very heavy losses. At first we had them fairly on the run, and had it not been for those inventions of the devil—machine guns and barbed wire—which suit the Turkish character and tactics to perfection, we should not have stopped short of the crest of Achi Baba. As it was, all brigades reported great numbers of dead Turks in front of their lines, and 350 prisoners were left in our hands.

On the 2nd, during the day, the enemy remained quiet, burying his dead under a red crescent flag, a work with which we did not interfere. Shortly after 9 p.m., however, they made another attack against the whole Allied line, their chief effort being made against the French front, where the ground favoured their approach. The attack was repulsed with loss.

During the night 3rd-4th the French front was again subjected to a heavy attack, which they were able to repulse without assistance from my general reserve.

The day of the 4th was spent in reorganisation, and a portion of the line held by the French, who had lost heavily during the previous night's fighting, was taken over by the 2nd Naval Brigade. The night passed quietly.

During the 5th the Lancashire Fusilier Brigade of the East Lancashire Division was disembarked and placed in reserve behind the British left.

Orders were issued for an advance to be carried out next day, and these and the three days' battle which ensued will be dealt with in my next despatch.

The losses, exclusive of the French, during the period covered by this despatch, were, I regret to say, very severe, numbering:—

177 Officers and 1,990 other ranks killed.
412 Officers and 7,807 other ranks wounded.
13 Officers and 3,580 other ranks missing.

From a technical point of view it is interesting to note that my Administrative Staff had not reached Mudros by the time when the landings were finally arranged. All the highly elaborate work involved by these landings was put through by my General Staff working in collaboration with Commodore Roger Kayes, C.B., M.V.O., and the Naval Transport Officers allotted for the purpose by Vice-Admiral de Robeck. Navy and Army carried out these combined duties with that perfect harmony which was indeed absolutely essential to success.

Throughout the events I have chronicled the Royal Navy has been father and mother to the Army. Not one of us but realises how much he owes to Vice-Admiral de Robeck; to the warships, French and British; to the destroyers, mine sweepers, picket boats, and to all their dauntless crews, who took no thought of themselves, but risked everything to give their soldier comrades a fair run in at the enemy.

Throughout these preparations and operations Monsieur le Général d'Amade has given me the benefit of his wide experiences of war, and has afforded me, always, the most loyal and energetic support. The landing of Kum Kale planned by me as a mere diversion to distract the attention of the enemy, was transformed by the Commander of the Corps Expéditionnaire de l'Orient into a brilliant operation, which secured some substantial results. During the fighting which followed the landing of the French Division at Sedd-el-Bahr no troops could have acquitted themselves more creditably under very trying circumstances, and under very heavy losses, than those working under the orders of Monsieur le Général d'Amade.

Lieutenant-General Sir W. R. Birdwood, K.C.S.I., C.B., C.I.E., D.S.O., was in command of the detached landing of the Australian and New Zealand Army Corps above Kaba Tepe, as well as during the subsequent fighting. The fact of his having been responsible for the execution of these difficult and hazardous operations, operations which were crowned with a very remarkable success, speaks, I think, for itself.

Major-General A. G. Hunter-Weston, C.B., D.S.O., was tried very highly, not only during the landings, but more especially in the day and night attacks and counter-attacks which ensued. Untiring, resourceful, and ever more cheerful as the outlook (on occasion) grew darker, he possesses, in my opinion, very special qualifications as a Commander of troops in the field.

Major-General W. P. Braithwaite, C.B., is the best Chief of the General Staff it has ever been my fortune to encounter in war. I will not pile epithets upon him. I can say no more than what I have said, and I can certainly say no less.

I have many other names to bring to notice for the period under review, and these will form the subject of a separate report at an early date.

I have the honour to be Your Lordship's most obedient Servant,

Ian Hamilton, General, Commanding Mediterranean Expeditionary Force.

THE END OF VOLUME IV

Edgar Wallace – A Short Biography

Richard Horatio Edgar Wallace was born on the 1st April 1875 at 7 Ashburnham Grove, Greenwich. His mother, Mary Jane "Polly" Richards was born into an Irish Catholic family in Liverpool in 1843 and had worked in theatres, both as an actress in bit-parts and as a stagehand and usherette, until she married a Merchant Navy Captain, Joseph Richards, in 1867. He too had been born into an Irish Catholic family in Liverpool. His father had also been a Captain in the Merchant Navy, and his mother's family had a marine background. Mary was eight months pregnant with Joseph's child when he died at sea, and it was once the child had been born that she first turned to the stage, taking the stage name Polly Richards.

She joined the Marriott family theatre troupe in 1872. It was managed by Mrs. Alice Edgar, Richard Edgar, Grace Edgar, Adeline Edgar and Richard Horatio Edgar, Wallace's father. In late 1874 Mary and Richard Horatio Edgar had a brief sexual encounter at the party following a successful show, and she fell pregnant. Worried about the scandal which would ensue and fearing that she might forever lose her job at the troupe, she fabricated an obligation in Greenwich would detain her there for at least six months. She lived in a room in the boarding house on Ashburnham Grove until her son, Edgar, was born. She had already made preparations through her midwife for a couple to foster the child, and when Edgar was born the midwife presented her with Mrs Freeman. Her husband was a fishmonger at Billingsgate market and she already had ten children. She was happy to foster the child and for Polly to make frequent visits to see him in exchange for a small sum of money which Polly made from her work in the theatre troupe.

Wallace was now known as Richard Horatio Edgar Freeman, taking his father's forenames and his foster family's surname. Broadly speaking his childhood was a happy one. The Freemans looked after him lovingly and he had good friendships with his foster siblings, particularly Clara Freeman, twenty years his senior, who often looked after him as a child. After a few years Polly's finances tightened and she was no longer in a position to afford the fee she had been paying the Freemans. However, they had grown to love the young Wallace and opted to adopt him in order to keep him out of the workhouse. Polly could no longer visit him. George Freeman was keen to ensure that he had equal opportunities and did all he could to secure him an education at St. Alfege with St. Peter's, a

Peckham boarding school. Despite his adoptive father's efforts, though, Wallace left the school aged twelve for truancy.

Instead he went to work and by the time he was fourteen or fifteen he had experience selling newspapers at Ludgate Circus, near Fleet Street, as a worker in a rubber factory, as a shoe shop assistant, as a milk delivery boy and as a ship's cook. He stole from the milk company which resulted in his dismissal, and in 1894 was engaged to a local girl from Deptford named Edith Anstree, though he broke this off and instead joined the Infantry. He adopted the name Edgar Wallace which he took from Lew Wallace, the author of *Ben-Hur*, and his medical record records a diminutive 33" chest and a stunted growth. his first posting was with the West Kent Regiment in South Africa in 1896, though he did not enjoy military life, arranging to be transferred to the Royal Army Medical Corps. Though this was a less strenuous job, it was also significantly less pleasant and so he again transferred to the Press Corps, which he found suited him far better.

He was in Cape Town in 1898 where he met Rudyard Kipling and was inspired to begin writing and publishing poetry and songs. His first collection of ballads, *The Mission that Failed!* and was enough of a success that in 1899 he paid his way out of the armed forces in order to turn to writing full time. His first work was as a war correspondent for Reuters who kept him in Africa to cover the Boer War, and then for the Daily Mail in 1900 and various other periodicals after that. It was while he was in South Africa that he met and married Ivy Maude Caldecott, who was 21 when they married in 1901, despite her Wesleyan missionary father's strong opposition to the union, for several reasons, one of which was that Wallace's writing was not turning quite the profit he had expected it would. *War and Other Poems* and *Writ in Barracks,* both published in 1900, had not proved as popular as his first collection. Eleanor Clare Hellier Wallace, their first child, died of meningitis in 1903 and, in rather deep debt, they returned to London. Wallace used his contacts with the Daily Mail to get work with them in London, electing to write detective novels as a means of making quick money.

Wallace met Polly, his birth mother, in 1903. He didn't remember her from his childhood as he had been too young when she became unable to visit, so it was as though they were meeting for the first time. She was sixty years old and terminally ill, living in abject poverty. She had come to Wallace seeking financial support, but he turned her away. She died in the Bradford Infirmary later that year. In 1904 he and Ivy had a son, Bryan. He was still writing and had completed his first thriller, *The Four Just Men.* Since nobody would publish it he resorted to setting up his own publishing company which he called Tallis Press and he published a serialised version of *The Four Just Men* in 1905. He received promotional assistance from the Daily Mail in which he ran a competition for entrants to guess the method of murder in the final chapter, with a prize of £1,000 for a correct guess. Although the paper's proprietor, Lord Alfred Harmsworth, refused Wallace the £1,000 prize money, Wallace persisted and went ahead with the competition, recklessly advertising on billboards and buses all over the country, hoping to expand his advertisements across the Empire. His worried colleagues at the Daily Mail managed to convince him to lower the prize money to £500, split into a first prize of £250, a second prize of £200 and a third of £50, but with the total cost of his advertisements nearing £2,000 he would need to sell £2,500 worth of copies before he could see any profit. He was confident that this could be achieved in just three months.

Though he had remarkable enthusiasm, it became clear that his managerial skills left a lot to be desired. It soon emerged that nowhere in the competition terms and conditions had he included a clause limiting the competition to one single winner; instead, any entrant with a winning answer was entitled to their corresponding prize money. Thus, if ten entrants guessed the first prize answer, the competition was obliged to pay each entrant £250. This error was only noticed after the competition had been closed and the solution had been printed in the final installment of the novel, meaning that not only was there no opportunity to write his way out of enormous financial obligation, but the entrants who had guessed correctly would by now have read the final chapter and know they had done so. £250 was an enormous amount of money to the average Edwardian family and those entitled to it were likely to make a lot of noise if they didn't receive their money. Despite this, Wallace's fist instinct was to attempt to ignore the issue entirely, even as he discovered that he initial calculations had been dramatically over-enthusiastic and it would take nearer to two years of continuous sales to break even at the initial cost of £2,500, let alone the new figure which included every correct guesser. Compounding the problem even further was the awful realisation that as sales continued throughout the initial three month period and Wallace approached the £2,500 break-even figure, new readers were still eligible to enter and guess correctly. Though it is unknown how much he eventually owed his readers, Lord Harmsworth found himself having to loan over £5,000 in order to protect the reputation of the newspaper, since 1906 had come around and there still hadn't been a list printed of all prize-winners. It was less a charitable act than one of a man anxious that the failure would reflect ill on his own paper. Wallace filed for bankruptcy shortly thereafter and as a token gesture to his creditors sold the rights to the novel to Sir George Newnes, a publisher and editor, for £75. In the midst of this chaos though, Wallace managed to write and published *Smithy*, which would become the first of a series of *Smithy* novels.

Following this fiascos Wallace was dismissed from the Daily Mail in 1907 when inaccuracies which were found in his reporting, resulting in libel cases being brought against the paper. That year he became the first reporter to be fired from the Daily Mail and was his awful reputation prevented him from finding work at any other papers. Despite all this, though, he travelled to the Congo Free State later that year and reported on the criminal treatment of the Congolese people by King Leopold II of Belgium and the Belgian rubber companies. Up to fifteen million Congolese were killed in various atrocities, and Wallace was asked to serialise stories based on his experiences for her penny magazine *Weekly Tale-Teller*. He and Ivy had another daughter, named Patricia, in 1908. Though his new work for *Weekly Tale-Teller* was bringing in some money, their financial situation was still dire and Ivy was occasionally forced to sell off her jewellery and possessions in order to pay for food. In 1911 his Congolese stories were published in a collection called *Sanders of the River*, which quickly became a bestseller. He would publish eleven more such collections featuring a total of 102 stories of adventure and tribal life set on the river Congo.

From 1908 he started to enjoy a revival of both his success and his reputation. The majority of his initial writing he sold outright in order to make money as quickly as possible and placate his creditors in the United Kingdom and South Africa, but as his success saw the reestablishment of his reputation he began to find work once again as a journalist, beginning in horse racing for the *Week-End*, the *Evening News* and then as an editor for the *Week-End Racing Supplement*. Following this success he started his own racing papers, *Bibury's* and *R. E. Walton's Weekly*, eventually buying his own racehorses and losing thousands gambling. His success was insufficient to support his newly extravagant lifestyle and his marriage began to fail in the light of his financial irresponsibility. He and Ivy had their last child together, Michael Blair Wallace, in 1916, and she filed for divorce in 1918 moving to Tunbridge Wells with her children.

Wallace began to fall for his secretary Ethel Violet King and they married in 1921, having a child, Penelope Wallace, in 1923, who would herself go on to become a successful crime writer. Wallace now began to take his career as a fiction writer more seriously, signing with Hodder and Stoughton in 1921. He now began to organize his contracts more carefully, arranging for royalties and properly organized promotions, run by people more business-minded than himself. He was marketed as the 'King of Thrillers' and they gave him the trademark image of a trilby, a cigarette holder and a yellow Rolls Royce. He was truly prolific, capable not only of producing a 70,000 word novel in three days but of doing three novels in a row in such a manner. His publishers signed off on almost everything he wrote as soon as he turned it in, estimating that by 1928 one in four books being read at any time was written by Wallace, for alongside his famous thrillers he wrote variously in other genres, including but not limited to science fiction, non-fiction accounts of WWI which amounted to ten volumes and screen plays. Eventually he would reach the remarkable total of 170 novels, 18 stage plays and 957 short stories.

Wallace became chairman of the Press Club which to this day holds an annual Edgar Wallace Award, rewarding 'excellence in writing'. In 1923 he broadcasted a report on the Epsom Derby horse race for the British Broadcasting Company, making him the first ever radio sports correspondent. His ex-wife Ivy had suffered from breast cancer between 1923-1924, and it eventually killed her in 1926 despite a successful operation to remove a tumour the year before. He wrote the essay "The Canker in our Midst" in 1926 which dealt, aggressively and controversially, with the problem of paedophilia in show business, describing how children were unwittingly left open to sexual abuse, and linking paedophilia with homosexuality. Its tone has been described as "intolerant, blustering, kick-the-blighters-down-the-stairs". He was appointed chairman of the British Lion Film Corporation on the back of the success of *The Ringer* and on the agreement that he give British Lion first choice on all his future work. This contract gave him an annual salary and a large amount of stock with the company, along with a stipend on all British Lion production of his work and 10% of their annual profits. This extraordinary contract gave him annual earnings by 1929 of almost £50,000, or almost £2 million in 2014.

He now became an active figure in politics, entering the 1931 general election as a Liberal contestant in Blackpool, rejecting the current government in favour of free trade. He lost the election by over 33,000 votes and went to America in late 1931, once again deeply in debt after buying the *Sunday News* which closed six months later. In America he quickly found work as a script doctor for RKO Pictures, enjoying early success with the 1932 adaptation of *The Hound of the Baskervilles*. This success, along with that of the play *The Green Pack*, established his reputation in America and he was able to see his own work adapted for film, beginning with *The Four Just Men*. His most successful theatrical work, *On The Spot*, which explores the life of Al Capone, has been described as "arguably, in construction, dialogue, action, plot and resolution, still one of the finest and purest of 20th-century melodramas". These successes led to his assignation on RKO's "gorilla picture" which would become famous as King Kong in 1933.

He worked on the first draft though he was beginning to experience severe headaches which brought about a diagnosis of diabetes. Despite taking medication to address his condition, it deteriorated in a matter of days. His wife booked him passage home but soon heard that he had entered a coma and died of his condition and double pneumonia on the 7th of February 1932 in North Maple Drive, Beverly Hills. In his honour the bell at St. Bride's church on Fleet Street tolled for the duration of the morning while the flags flew at half-mast. He was buried near his home in England at Chalklands, Bourne End, in Buckinghamshire. Once again, at the time of his death he was in severe debt, mostly to racing bookkeepers, though these debts were settled within two years thanks to the enormous royalties his estate continued to receive from his contracts. His writing has been translated into 29 languages, and is considered one of the most important bodies of Colonial writing.

Edgar Wallace – A Concise Bibliography

African Novels
Sanders of the River (1911)
The People of the River (1911)
The River of Stars (1913)

Bosambo of the River (1914)
Bones (1915)
The Keepers of the King's Peace (1917)
Lieutenant Bones (1918)
Bones in London (1921)
Sandi the Kingmaker (1922)
Bones of the River (1923)
Sanders (1926)
Again Sanders (1928)

Four Just Men (Series)
The Four Just Men (1905)
The Council of Justice (1908)
The Just Men of Cordova (1917)
The Law of the Four Just Men (US title: Again the Three Just Men) (1921)
The Three Just Men (1926)
Again the Three Just Men (US title: The Law of the Three Just Men) (1929) a.k.a. Again the Three

Mr. J. G. Reeder (Series)
Room 13 (1924)
The Mind of Mr. J. G. Reeder (US title: The Murder Book of Mr. J. G. Reeder) (1925)
Terror Keep (1927)
Red Aces (1929)[27]
The Guv'nor and Other Short Stories (US title: Mr. Reeder Returns) (1932)

Detective Sgt. (Inspector) Elk series
The Nine Bears or The Other Man or The Cheaters (1910)
revised as Silinski - Master Criminal (1930)
The Fellowship of the Frog (1925)
The Joker or The Colossus (1926)
The Twister (1928)
The India-Rubber Men (1929)
White Face (1930)

Educated Evans (Series)
Educated Evans (1924)
More Educated Evans (1926)
Good Evans (1927)

Smithy (Series)
Smithy (1905)
Smithy Abroad (1909)
Smithy and The Hun (1915)
Nobby or Smithy's Friend Nobby (1916)

Crime Novels
Angel Esquire (1908)
The Fourth Plague or Red Hand (1913)
Grey Timothy or Pallard the Punter (1913)
The Man Who Bought London (1915)
The Melody of Death (1915)

A Debt Discharged (1916)
The Tomb of T'Sin (1916)
The Secret House (1917)
The Clue of the Twisted Candle (1918)
Down under Donovan (1918)
The Man Who Knew (1918)
The Strange Lapses of Larry Loman (1918)
The Green Rust (1919)
Kate Plus Ten (1919)
The Daffodil Mystery or The Daffodil Murder (1920)
Jack O'Judgment (1920)
The Angel of Terror or The Destroying Angel (1922)
The Crimson Circle (1922)
Mr. Justice Maxwell or Take-A-Chance Anderson(1922)
The Valley of Ghosts (1922)
Captains of Souls (1923)
The Clue of the New Pin (1923)
The Green Archer (1923)
The Missing Million (1923)
The Dark Eyes of London or The Croakers (1924)
Double Dan or Diana of Kara-Kara (US Title) (1924)
The Face in the Night or The Diamond Men or The Ragged Princess (1924)
The Sinister Man (1924)
The Three Oak Mystery (1924)
The Blue Hand or Beyond Recall (1925)
The Daughters of the Night (1925)
The Gaunt Stranger or Police Work (1925) revised as The Ringer (1926)
A King by Night (1925)
The Strange Countess (1925)
The Avenger or The Hairy Arm (1926)
'The Black Abbot (1926)
The Day of Uniting (1926)
The Door with Seven Locks (1926)
The Man from Morocco or Souls In Shadows or The Black (US Title) (1926)
The Million Dollar Story (1926)
The Northing Tramp or The Tramp (1926)
Penelope of the Polyantha (1926)
The Square Emerald or The Woman (1926)
The Terrible People or The Gallows' Hand (1926)
We Shall See! or The Gaol-Breakers (US Title) (1926)
The Yellow Snake or The Black Tenth (1926)
Big Foot (1927)
The Feathered Serpent or Inspector Wade or Inspector Wade and the Feathered Serpent (1927)
Flat 2 (1927)
The Forger or The Counterfeiter (1927)
Terror Keep (1927)
The Hand of Power or The Proud Sons of Ragusa (1927)
The Man Who Was Nobody (1927)
Number Six (1927)
The Squeaker or The Sign of the Leopard or The Squealer (US Title) (1927)
The Traitor's Gate (1927)

The Double (1928)
The Flying Squad (1928)
The Gunner or Gunman's Bluff (US Title) (1928)
Four Square Jane or The Fourth Square (1929)
The Golden Hades or Stamped In Gold or The Sinister Yellow Sign (1929)
The Green Ribbon (1929)
The Calendar (1930)
The Clue of the Silver Key or The Silver Key (1930)
The Lady of Ascot (1930)
The Devil Man or Sinister Street or Silver Steel
or The Life and Death of Charles Peace (1931)
The Man at the Carlton or The Mystery of Mary Grier (1931)
The Coat of Arms or The Arranways Mystery (1931)
On the Spot: Violence and Murder in Chicago (1931)
When the Gangs Came to London or Scotland Yard's Yankee Dick
or The Gangsters Come To London (1932)
The Frightened Lady or The Case of the Frightened Lady or Criminal At Large (1933)
The Green Pack (1933)
The Man Who Changed His Name (1935)
The Mouthpiece (1935)
Smoky Cell (1935)
The Table (1936)
Sanctuary Island (1936)

Other Novels
Captain Tatham of Tatham Island or Eve's Island or The Island of Galloping Gold (1909)
The Duke in the Suburbs (1909)
Private Selby (1912)
"1925" - The Story of a Fatal Peace (1915)
Those Folk of Bulboro (1918)
The Book of all Power (1921)
Flying Fifty-five (1922)
The Books of Bart (1923)
Barbara on Her Own (1926)

Poetry Collections
The Mission That Failed (1898)
War and Other Poems (1900)
Writ In Barracks (1900)

Non-Fiction
Unofficial Despatches of the Anglo-Boer War (1901)
Famous Scottish Regiments (1914)
Field Marshal Sir John French (1914)
Heroes All: Gallant Deeds of the War (1914)
The Standard History of the War – Volumes 1 – 4 (1914)
Kitchener's Army and the Territorial Forces:
The Full Story of a Great Achievement (1915)
Vol. 2-4. War of the Nations (1915)
Vol. 5-7. War of the Nations (1916)
Vol. 8-9. War of the Nations (1917)

Famous Men and Battles of the British Empire (1917)
Tam of the Scouts (1918)
The Real Shell-Man: The Story of Chetwynd of Chilwell (1919)
People or Edgar Wallace by Himself(1926)
The Trial of Patrick Herbert Mahon (1928)
My Hollywood Diary (1932)

Screenplays
King Kong (1932, first draft of original screenplay, 110 pages) While the script was not used in its
entirety, much of it was retained for the final screenplay.
The Hound of the Baskervilles (1932, British film)
The Squeaker (1930, British film)
Prince Gabby (1929, British film)
Mark of the Frog (1928, American film)
The Valley of Ghosts (192

Short Story Collections
The Admirable Carfew (1914)
The Adventure of Heine (1917)
Tam O' the Scouts (1918)
The Fighting Scouts (1919)
Chick (1923)
The Black Avons (1925)
The Brigand (1927)
The Mixer (1927)
This England (1927)
The Orator (1928)
The Thief in the Night (1928)
Elegant Edward (1928)
The Lone House Mystery and Other Stories (Collins and son, 1929)
The Governor of Chi-Foo (1929)
Again the Ringer The Ringer Returns (US Title) (1929)
The Big Four or Crooks of Society (1929)
The Black or Blackmailers I Have Foiled (1929)
The Cat-Burglar (1929)
Circumstantial Evidence (1929)
Fighting Snub Reilly (1929)
For Information Received (1929)
Forty-Eight Short Stories (1929)
Planetoid 127 and The Sweizer Pump (1929)
The Ghost of Down Hill & The Queen of Sheba's Belt (1929)
The Iron Grip (1929)
The Lady of Little Hell (1929)
The Little Green Man (1929)
The Prison-Breakers (1929)
The Reporter (1929)
Killer Kay (1930)
Mrs William Jones and Bill (1930)
Forty Eight Short-Stories (George Newnes Limited ca. 1930)
The Stretelli Case and Other Mystery Stories (1930)
The Terror (1930)

The Lady Called Nita (1930)
Sergeant Sir Peter or Sergeant Dunn, C.I.D. (1932)
The Scotland Yard Book of Edgar Wallace (1932)
The Steward (1932)
Nig-Nog and other humorous stories (1934)
The Last Adventure (1934)
The Woman From the East (1934) Co-written By Robert George Curtis
The Edgar Wallace Reader of Mystery and Adventure (1943)
The Undisclosed Client (1963)

Other
King Kong, with Draycott M. Dell, (1933), 28 October 1933 Cinema Weekly

Plays
An African Millionaire (1904)
The Forest of Happy Dreams (1910)
Dolly Cutting Herself (1911)
The Manager's Dream (1914)
M'Lady (1921)
Double Dan (1926)
The Mystery of room 45 (1926)
A Perfect Gentleman (1927)
The Terror (1927)
Traitors Gate (1927)
The Lad (1928)
The Man Who Changed His Name (1928)
The Squeaker (1928)[27]
The Calendar (1929)
Persons Unknown (1929)
The Ringer (1929)
The Mouthpiece (1930)
On the Spot (1930)
Smoky Cell (1930)
The Squeaker (1930)
To Oblige A Lady (1930)
The Case of the Frightened Lady (1931)
The Old Man (1931)
The Green Pack (1932)
The Table (1932)

www.ingramcontent.com/pod-product-compliance
Lightning Source LLC
Chambersburg PA
CBHW060051050426
42448CB00011B/2396